Machine-Stitched
Cathedral Windows
Updating an Old Favorite

SHELLEY SWANLAND

Martingale
& C O M P A N Y

BOTHELL, WASHINGTON

To Rob, Becky, Sybill, Raymond, Valerie, Kelby, Leslie, and Carol.

❖

ACKNOWLEDGMENTS

I am very grateful to my family for all of their patience, love, and support. I also appreciate the support and encouragement of all my friends from Shady Ladies, SLO Quilters, SLO Rags, Quilt Camp, Sew Gently, and Betty's Fabrics.

CREDITS

President . . . . Nancy J. Martin
CEO/Publisher . . . . Daniel J. Martin
Associate Publisher . . . . Jane Hamada
Editorial Director . . . . Mary V. Green
Design and Production Manager . . . . Cheryl Stevenson
Technical Editor . . . . Laurie Baker
Copy Editor . . . . Liz McGehee
Illustrator . . . . Laurel Strand
Cover Design . . . . Rohani Design
Text Design . . . . Trina Stahl
Photographer . . . . Brent Kane

Machine-Stitched Cathedral Windows: Updating an Old Favorite
© 1999 by Shelley Swanland

Martingale & Company
PO Box 118
Bothell, WA 98041-0118 USA
www.patchwork.com

Printed in China
04 03 02 01 00   6 5 4 3 2 1

That Patchwork Place is an imprint of Martingale & Company.

MISSION STATEMENT

We are dedicated to providing quality products and service by working together to inspire creativity and to enrich the lives we touch.

Library of Congress Cataloging-in-Publication Data

Swanland, Shelley, 1952–
    Machine-stitched cathedral windows : updating an old favorite / Shelley Swanland.
        p.   cm.
    ISBN 1-56477-285-3
    1. Patchwork Patterns.   2. Machine sewing.   I. Title.
II. Title: Cathedral windows.
TT835.S86   1999
746.46'041—dc21   99-44334
                                                          CIP

Contents

❖

INTRODUCTION

❖

IF YOU HAVE always loved Cathedral Window quilts but thought them too difficult or time-consuming, then you will be as excited as I am about this new approach. Although they look like old-fashioned Cathedral Window quilts, these quilts are made using a completely different method of construction. I call it the Foundation Grid Method.

Unlike traditional methods where each piece is sewn by hand, this technique lets you construct the entire quilt by machine. But this technique isn't just about being able to machine stitch the pieces together. What makes this technique different is the way the pieces go together. First, the seams of the window frames are machine sewn into an underlying grid that forms the foundation of the entire quilt top. The quilt top is then layered over the batting and backing. Next, the window panes are positioned, and the folded edges of the frames are pulled over the raw edges of the window panes, tacked, and quilted by machine.

While this may all seem like a puzzle now, once you complete the first frame piece, I guarantee the light bulb will go on and you'll never use another method to complete a Cathedral Window quilt again. Even if you prefer hand stitching, this method will save you time.

In addition to saving time, there are other advantages to this method. Fabric choices can be varied on three different levels: the background, the window frames, and the window panes. While this alone allows for an infinite number of fabric combinations, the grid style also can be changed, opening the door to even more possibilities.

Before I discovered the Foundation Grid Method, I had never been able to complete a Cathedral Window quilt, so you can see why I'm so excited. I hope you, too, will be just as excited. Have fun experimenting with colors and patterns, and enjoy your quilts!

GENERAL INSTRUCTIONS

❖

*W*ITHIN THESE GENERAL instructions, you will find the guidelines necessary to construct a successful final project, so this is not a chapter you can skip. All of the quilt instructions follow the basic principles of assembling a square-frame quilt, so I advise mastering that section before venturing into more advanced shapes.

Cutting the Pieces

THERE ARE THREE major pieces used to assemble a Cathedral Window quilt: foundation pieces, frame pieces, and pane pieces.

It is important to follow the grain lines noted on all the window-frame patterns. The frame edges that will be folded over the window panes must be on the bias so they will stretch and lie flat. Grain line is not as critical when cutting the foundation pieces, but you do need to be consistent in your cutting. If the frame pieces are even slightly larger than the templates, you will catch the folds in the foundation seams.

You may want to wait until the foundation pieces are together before cutting the window panes. This will give you a better indication of how they will look with the foundation and frames. Window panes (indicated by a *WP* on the template) are cut about ¼" smaller on all sides than the frame they will fit, and the edges will not be turned under. The window panes are not attached until the quilt layers are basted. Use the lines marked on the matching frame templates to position the window panes on the frames at that time.

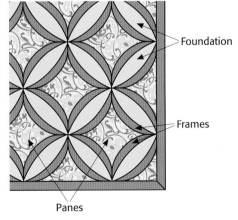

Foundation

Frames

Panes

Use rotary-cutting equipment to do as much of the cutting as possible. When cutting squares or rectangles, it is the quickest and easiest way. Be sure the blade on your rotary cutter is sharp so it cuts completely through the fabric. Uncut threads holding your pieces together can lead to distortion. For pieces that are not square or rectangular, use a pair of good-quality, sharp scissors.

Instructions detailing the cutting sequence accompany each quilt. If templates are used, copy the templates onto template plastic, then follow the order of cutting for the least amount of waste. Be sure to cut only the number of pieces needed, because the extra fabric is sometimes used for other pieces. When cutting a reverse piece (indicated by an *r* following the template letter, i.e., *Hr*), alternate the right and wrong side of the fabric, or flip the pattern over and cut each piece individually.

Whenever possible, I recommend cutting a strip and then cutting the individual pieces from the strip. Cut all strips across the width of the fabric unless otherwise indicated. To save time, cut several layers together. Place the pattern piece on the strip and mark all edges, nesting the pieces whenever possible. Cut all outer edges with the rotary cutter if possible. The inside angles can then be cut with scissors.

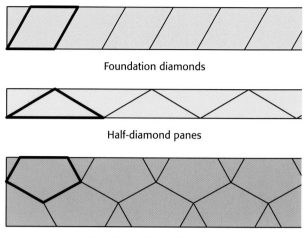

Foundation diamonds

Half-diamond panes

Short half-diamond frames

When cutting a large number of unusual shapes, such as diamonds and hexagons, it is easier to create a grid. Trace the shapes onto the desired fabric, using the plastic template and a sharp pencil. Move across the fabric until no more shapes will fit, lining up each shape with the sides or side points touching. Nest the next row against the first one; continue in this manner until the number of shapes required for each quilt are traced. Pin the marked fabric on top of multiple layers of the frame fabric, and then cut out the shapes with scissors.

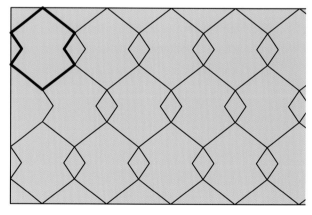

Diamond frames

The hexagon-shaped triangle frames, Templates R and S, used in "Garden Windows," are a little tricky to cut. None of the six sides of the hexagon can be on the straight grain, or one of the folded frame edges will not be bias. To properly cut the shapes, lay out a line of Template R as shown, making sure the template grain line follows the fabric grain line. Using your rotary cutter and ruler, make the first cut of the fabric off-grain. Cut the necessary number of strips, using this off-grain edge as your starting point. Pin several layers of strips together, placing the marked strip on top, and cut out the pieces.

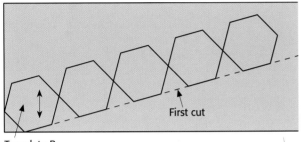

First cut

Template R

Assembling the Foundation and Frames

ONE OF THE greatest benefits of the Foundation Grid Method is that the grid can be changed to create new shapes. The classic Square On-Point uses a foundation of squares, but change the squares to rectangles and the frame shape becomes a diamond. "Denim Diamonds" (see page 31) and "Gothic Windows" (see page 34) are two examples. Change the grid to a combination of squares and diamonds, and new geometric shapes, such as kites and trapezoids, are created. These frame shapes are used in combination with square and diamond frames to form the more complex design layouts found in "Mystical Windows", "Starry Night", "Cathedral Heart", and "Celestial View". The last three quilts featured use an isometric grid. "Garden Windows" uses foundation diamonds and triangle frames to create hexagons visually, while "Tumbling Windows" and "Tumbling Stars" use a foundation wedge and diamond frames to do the same.

SQUARE FRAMES

Option 1—Work Around the Block

1. Using the frame and foundation square sizes required for 1 of the first 3 quilts, cut at least 1 strip of each.

2. Start with 4 foundation pieces and 1 square frame. Fold the square frame in half, wrong sides together, forming a rectangle. With the short end up and the raw edges to the left, place the rectangle between 2 foundation pieces, right sides together. Line up the upper edge and left-side raw edges. The foundation piece will extend ¼" from the frame fold on the right-hand side. Pin through all 4 layers on the fold and ⅜" to ½" from the left edge.

3. With the fold of the frame facing you, backstitch to the first pin, then stitch right up to the second pin, using a ¼" seam allowance. Take 1 stitch over the pin and backstitch.

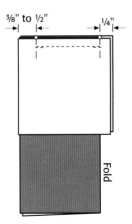

⅜" to ½" ¼"

Fold

TIPS

- Never sew over other seams.
- Always backstitch at the beginning and end of each seam.
- Always start sewing at the raw edge and stitch toward the fold.

4. Rotate the block counterclockwise and open it out so you can see the wrong side of the frame fabric. Fold the lower right corner of the frame up to the seam upper edge. Lay a foundation square on top. Match the 4 corners; pin and stitch as shown in step 3.

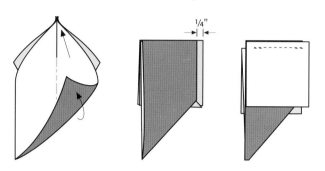

5. Repeat the rotating, pinning, and sewing process for the third seam.

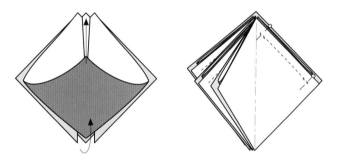

6. Bring the unsewn edges of the first and fourth foundation squares together, keeping the foundation-square folded edge to the right as shown. Stitch as shown in step 3.

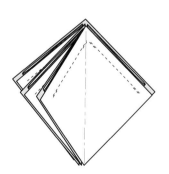

7. Now, flatten the 4 foundation squares. This will pull the frame block into a square set on-point with folded bias edges. Turn it over and you will see the 4-square foundation grid.

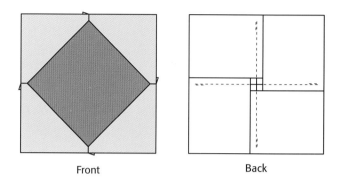

Front   Back

8. Now it is time to add another frame. I will address corner frames and edge frames shortly, but first, let's sew a few internal frames together. The 2 raw edges of each foundation square will become 2 seams of an adjacent frame. Start with the upper left corner of your assembled frame block. Fold a new frame square in half, wrong sides together, and lay it on the frame block, aligning the fold with the center seam allowance, and the raw edges with the left side of the completed block. Lay a foundation square over the frame fabric; pin and sew as described earlier.

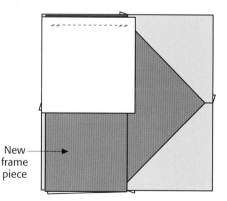

New frame piece

9. Work around this frame in the same manner as before until all 4 seams are sewn. Additional frames will be added based on the individual quilt diagram.

TIP

THE FOLDED EDGE of the frame always meets the center seam allowance of another folded frame edge, and the raw edges always line up with the raw edges of the foundation corners. There are no rules as far as the order in which they are sewn. My personal preference when sewing squares and rectangles is to start at the lower left corner of the quilt top and work in diagonal rows. As each frame is added diagonally, it lines up horizontally with another frame. When this happens, the next frame is sewn between the two foundation squares that meet, and only two new foundation squares need to be added to each frame.

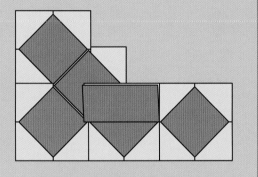

Some of the quilts work better if they're constructed from the center out. I have recommended my preference in the individual quilt instructions. Check your work frequently if you are following a complex design.

Option 2—Sew Opposite Seams First

1. Referring to steps 2 and 3 of Option 1, stitch the foundation and frame pieces together.

2. Repeat the procedure to stitch the remaining 2 foundation pieces to the opposite end of the frame piece.

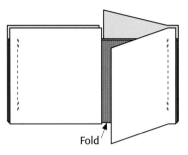

3. Grasp the seam allowances and push them together until they meet; pin.

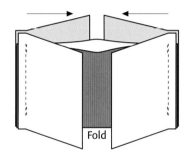

4. Sew the remaining seams individually. Be careful not to sew across the center seam.

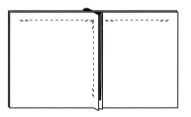

5. Continue adding frames as instructed in Option 1, step 8, sewing opposite seams as before.

Adding Edge Frames

No matter which option you selected for sewing the foundation and frames together, all of the open seams on the edge of the quilt will need to be sewn.

1. Fold the edge-frame piece in half, wrong sides together, to form a square. Lay the edge-frame fold against the seam that runs parallel to the edge, as shown, matching the raw edges.

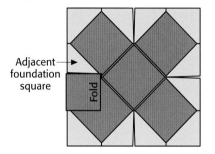

At this point, if there is an adjacent foundation square, fold it over the edge-frame square, right sides together. If there is no adjacent foundation square, place one over the edge-frame square, right sides together. Stitch from the fold to the opposite edge. Backstitch at the beginning and end.

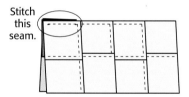

2. Open out the edge frame and finger-press it in place. The folded edges nearest the raw edge should cross adjoining folds and seams. Stitch along the raw edge.

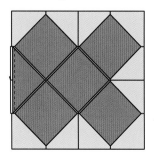

Adding Corner Frames

There are two kinds of corners used in these quilts, depending on the layout—single-corner frames and double-corner frames.

When a single-corner frame is called for, fold the frame square in half diagonally. Lay it on the corner, butting folded edges and aligning raw edges. Sew along the two raw edges, pivoting at the corner.

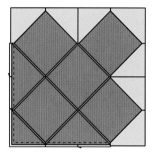

A double-corner frame is simply two edge frames that meet at the corner. Sew each edge frame into its respective seam. Finger-press, then pin each frame in place. Stitch along the edges, pivoting at the corner.

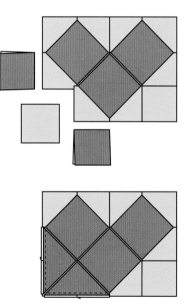

DIAMOND AND COMBINATION FRAMES

When the designs use a combination of rectangles and squares in the grid, geometric shapes such as diamond, kite, and trapezoid frames, are formed.

The method for handling the construction of these frames is basically the same as the square designs. The lengths of the seams vary, but they will still be straight. They all have four foundation seams that meet beneath each frame.

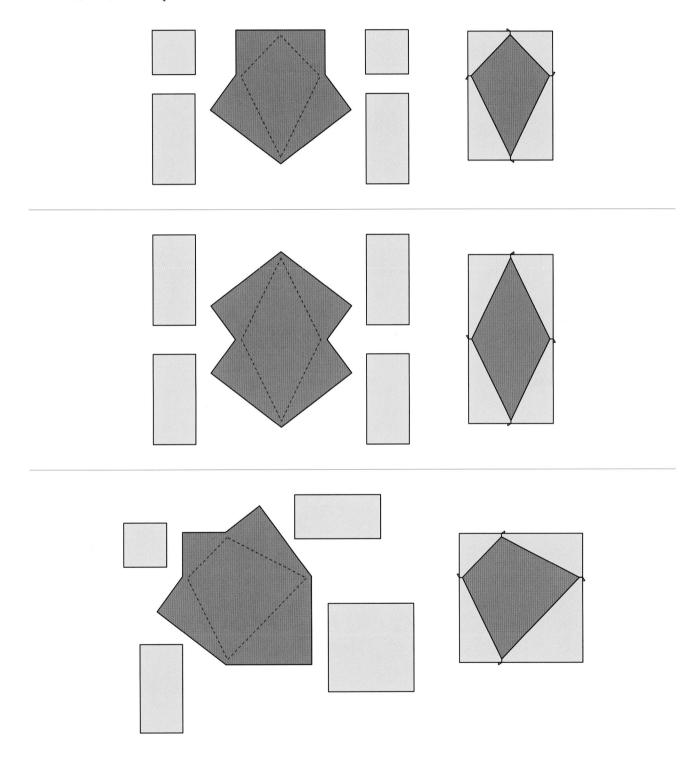

When using diamonds, kites, and trapezoid frames, the long sides of the frames will match the long sides of the foundation pieces. The same is true for the short sides. When working with frames that have long sides, it is sometimes easier to sew the longer seams first. Watch both the foundation shapes and the frame shapes as you work through the quilt plan. Check the quilt plan often as you add the frames. If you become confused, just fold the frame corners to the center, and the finished shape will emerge. Compare it to the pieces already sewn and you should be able to visualize the correct placement.

ISOMETRIC GRID FRAMES

Garden Windows

"Garden Windows" uses a diamond foundation grid and triangle frames. When turned over, you will see there are only three intersecting foundation seams beneath each frame. You can see in the photo on page 56 how six foundation pieces visually form a hexagon.

The technique for stitching this foundation is the same as for square-foundation quilts, but this time you'll be using diamond-shaped foundation pieces and hexagon-shaped frames. Fold the hexagon frame in half and stitch it between two diamond foundation pieces.

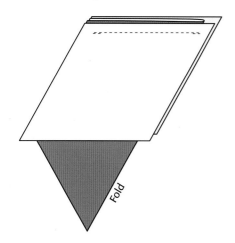

Open out the frame, fold the lower edge up, and add the last frame piece to complete the block.

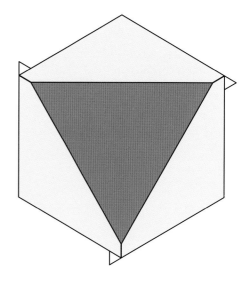

Be very careful with the grain line on this one. Refer to the instructions starting on page 5 for specific cutting details.

Tumbling Windows and Tumbling Stars

Both of these designs use a diamond frame on a wedge-shaped foundation. When the piece is turned over, note the four intersecting seams. The deeper points of the diamond frame will intersect in groups of six.

1. Fold the frame piece in half lengthwise. Place it between 2 wedge-shaped foundation pieces, right sides together, as shown. Place pins through all layers at the frame fold edge and ⅜" to ½" from the left edge. Stitch from pin to pin, backstitching at each end. Repeat for the opposite long edge.

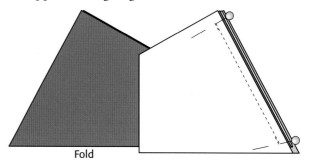

Fold

2. Turn the piece so that 1 stitched edge is facing you. Open out the frame fabric and align the 2 stitched foundation seams. Pin the short edges together. Sew each side separately, being careful that the frame piece is folded so only the raw edges are stitched into the seam.

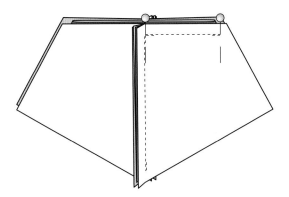

3. Flatten the foundation pieces to pull the frame into a diamond.

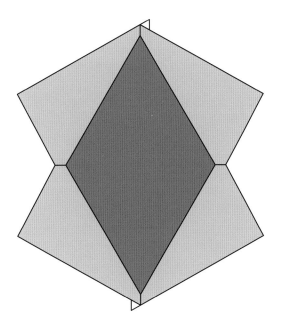

Pressing

PRESSING IS A critical element in determining how flat the quilt top will lie. For best results, press from the wrong side, beginning at one edge of the quilt and working out. Press seams to one side in a spiral around each intersection. The direction of the spiral will alternate from one intersection to the next. Pull the quilt top flat as you go and the frames will automatically be pulled into their correct position. I like to spray the seams with a little water as I press. Just be careful not to distort the piece if you use steam.

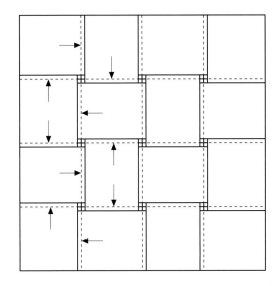

Adding Borders

BEFORE ADDING THE borders, pin the edge panes and corner panes to their corresponding frames. The raw edge of the panes will then be sewn into the border seam.

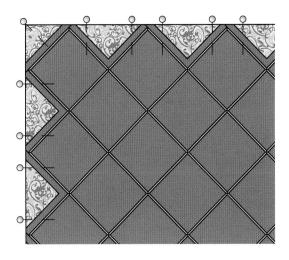

Borders can be mitered or sewn Log Cabin style. I have used both for the quilts in this book.

Mitered Borders

1. If there is more than one border, sew the border strips together lengthwise and treat them as one for this process. Press a crease at the center point of the top, bottom, and side border strips.

2. Lay the quilt top on a flat surface and gently smooth it out. Measure from side to side through the center and from top to bottom through the center. Try not to stretch the foundation. Check and recheck until you are sure the measurement is correct.

3. On each border strip, measure out from the center point exactly half the measurement of the edge you are stitching. Measure ¼" in from each mark and make another mark.

4. With the border strips on top and right sides together, line up the border-strip center point with the quilt-top center point, and the quilt corners with the border-strip outer marks; pin in place.

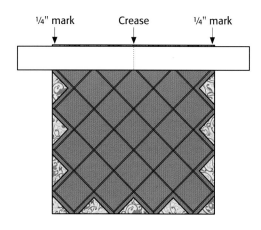

5. Using a ¼" seam, backstitch to the first ¼" mark, then sew to the next ¼" mark and backstitch. Be careful to keep the seams of the foundation lying in the direction they were pressed. Check and re-sew if necessary.

6. To miter the corners, fold the quilt diagonally so that the borders lie on top of each other, matching the border edges. Line up the 45°

line on the ruler with the straight edge of the border. The edge of the ruler should line up with the ¼" mark and extend out and away from the quilt. Flip your ruler over if necessary. Carefully mark along the edge of the ruler.

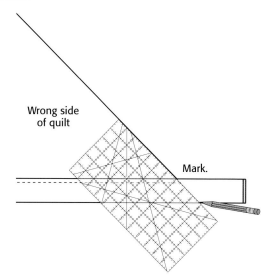

7. Pin the two borders together, carefully matching seams and edges. Sew on the marked line, backstitching at the ¼" mark. Trim the seams to ¼". Press the seams toward the side borders. Repeat for the remaining corners.

Log Cabin Borders

1. Lay the quilt top on a flat surface and gently smooth it out. Measure, being careful not to stretch the foundation, across the quilt center from top to bottom, raw edge to raw edge. Cut 2 side border strips the exact length measured and the width indicated in the instructions.

2. Pin the strips to the sides of the quilt top, then sew, using ¼" seams. Sew slowly. Keep the panes lined up and make sure the seam allowances of the foundation grid lie in the direction they were pressed. As you finish each border strip, check for any errant seam allowances and re-sew if necessary. Press the seams toward the border.

3. Repeat this process for the top and bottom borders, carefully measuring across the center of the quilt from side to side, including the side borders you just added. Cut the remaining 2 border strips to the exact measurement. Pin and sew, backstitching at the raw edges. Press the seams toward the border.

Piecing the Backing

IF THE MEASUREMENT of your quilt back, including the excess needed for take-up during quilting, is larger than one width of your backing fabric, you will need to piece a backing. When piecing a backing, be sure to balance what you add. In other words, instead of having a seam down the middle of the quilt where two fabrics are joined, add equal amounts to the sides of one width of fabric.

Basting the Quilt

AT THIS POINT, you are ready to baste the quilt layers together.

1. Spread your backing on a flat surface, right side down, and tape or clip it to the surface so it won't slide or buckle. Layer the batting over the backing and then the quilt top, right side up, over the batting. Smooth out the layers. The backing and batting should be a few inches larger all the way around the quilt top.

2. Starting at the center and working out, pin-baste with safety pins. If there are window pane pieces, place them on top of each frame first and then pin-baste. I prefer size 2 or curved safety pins. You will have to pin slightly off-center to avoid the thickest area. Use 2 pins for the larger frames.

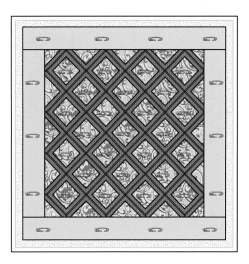

Tacking the Frames

AT EACH CORNER of the window frame, you will be pulling back the edges of the frame and covering the corner and edges of the window pane.

Set your sewing machine for a bar tack. If you have a computerized machine, program a tacking stitch into the memory. Drop your feed dogs or cover them. Set the stitch length to 0 and your stitch width to about 2.5. Bartack at the point the frame sides touch but do not cross, catching each side of the frame. The deeper the angle of the frame corner, the deeper the point at which they will cross. Move across the quilt from one corner to the next without cutting your threads. Work in one direction at a time so you don't need to turn the quilt. Do not tack the frame edges that are sewn into the borders.

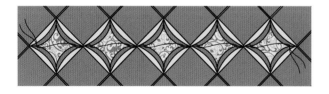

When you are finished tacking in one direction, trim the top threads and then the back threads. Don't tug too hard or you will pull the threads out.

Quilting the Frames and Borders

THE QUILTING IS accomplished by stitching down the frame edges that have been pulled over the pane edges. You can do this by straight stitching on the frame edge. You can also use a buttonhole or blind hem stitch just off the edge, catching the frame edge with the side stitches.

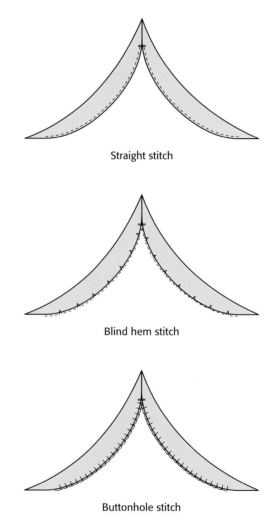

Straight stitch

Blind hem stitch

Buttonhole stitch

The frames pull back and lie down fairly consistently. You do not need to pin them. As you sew, gently push or pull the edge toward the center of the frame. Be careful not to pull it too much or you will create pulls at the corners. Likewise, if you do not push it enough, it will create a tuck at the end of the stitching line.

Stitch from one tack to the next. I usually take just one stitch over the tack, which is normally at the center point, leave the needle down, and pivot. On the smaller quilts, I stitch all the way around each frame, turning the quilt as I go and backstitching at the beginning and end. This is too much work on the larger quilts. On those, I work in rows across the quilt, backstitching at each corner. When you finish stitching in one direction, trim the threads or they will get in your way.

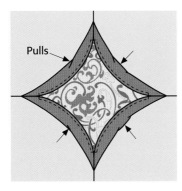

Too much tension

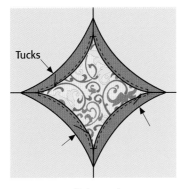

Too little tension

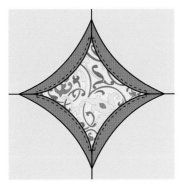

Perfect tension—
no tucks, no pulls

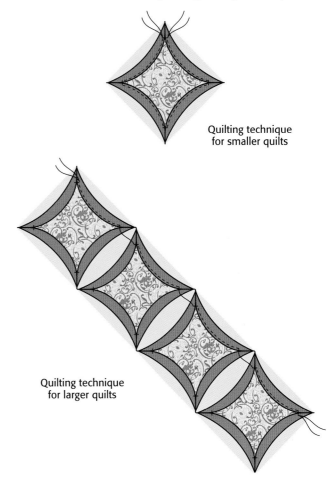

Quilting technique
for smaller quilts

Quilting technique
for larger quilts

If the quilt has borders, quilt right up to the borders. When you quilt the frame edges by the borders, start at one point and work your way all around the quilt without cutting the thread. Remember that you didn't tack these corners. Just lay the frame edges up against the border seam and stitch them down. Be careful not to lap them over the border seam, but be sure they touch the border, or the raw edges of the pane will show.

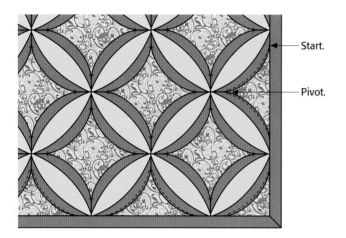

Start.

Pivot.

Quilt the borders as you would any other quilt. A few ideas are included with the individual quilts.

If the quilt does not have borders, wait until you have sewn on the binding before you quilt the edge frames. Quilt the edges as discussed earlier, then hand sew the binding to the back as described on the following pages.

Finishing the Quilt

USE YOUR FAVORITE method to cut binding strips for the quilt edges. Sometimes I cut my bindings on the bias; sometimes I don't. Be sure to cut several inches more than the total of the finished edges of the quilt.

CUTTING BIAS BINDING

STRIPS FOR BIAS binding are cut on the bias grain of the fabric. For the quilts in this book, I have suggested ¾ to ⅞ of a yard of fabric, depending on the quilt.

Straighten the raw edges of the fabric with the rotary cutter. Cut off the selvage. Fold one short edge of the fabric diagonally so that it meets the adjacent raw edge. Lay your ruler along the fold, and trim off just the very edge of the fold.

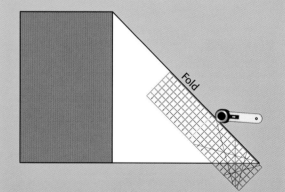

Set aside the fabric triangle. Cut 3"-wide strips from this bias edge. You will need twice the quilt length, plus twice the quilt width, plus about 4" extra. Sew the strips together using diagonal seams.

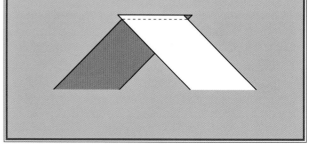

To stitch the binding to the quilt, follow these directions:

1. Cut 2 strips, each slightly longer than the length of the quilt. Fold them in half length-wise, wrong sides together, and press.

2. Place the binding on the quilt top, aligning the binding raw edges with the quilt raw edges. Stitch, using a ¼" seam allowance.

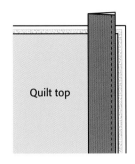

3. Trim the backing and batting ½" from the stitching line. Press the binding toward the edges.

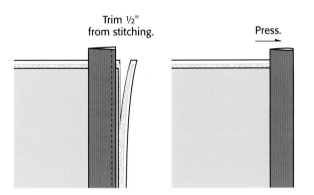

4. Measure the width of the quilt, including the binding you just added, and repeat the process for the top and bottom. Trim the backing and batting ½" from the stitching line. Trim the binding ends ¼" from the folded edge of the side binding. Press the binding toward the edges.

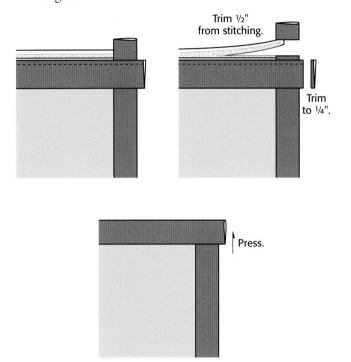

5. Quilt the edge frames.

6. Starting with the sides, fold the edge of the binding to the back and slipstitch it in place. The ends of the top and bottom binding will automatically fold in. Clip any bulk from the corners, fold the binding edges to the back, and slipstitch into place.

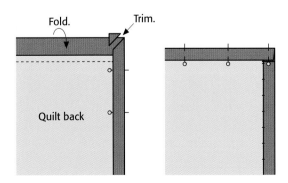

Clip the corner and fold the binding to the back.

CREATING A TRADITIONAL LOOK

*T*HE QUILTS IN this section are the most basic and also the most similar looking to the old-fashioned version of a Cathedral Windows quilt. The foundation is formed on a grid of squares that are half the size of the squares used to form the frames. The only difference in the basic design of these three quilts is the size of the squares used. Of course, the fabrics you choose and the way you arrange them will make a big difference in the finished quilt, too.

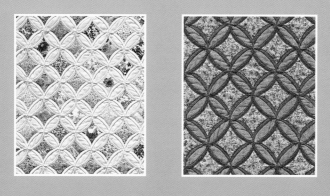

Classic Windows

CLASSIC WINDOWS, *1998, 49" x 57". The look of the traditional Cathedral Windows design is reflected in this version that uses the Foundation Grid Method. By using the same fabric for the foundation and frame pieces and multiple fabrics for the window panes, the old-fashioned scrappy look emerges.*

MATERIALS: *42"-wide fabric*

Piece	Fabric	Total Yardage Required	First Cut	Second Cut
Foundation	Natural Muslin	3¼ yds.	42 strips, 2½" x 42"	672 squares, 2½" x 2½"
Window Frames	Natural Muslin	5½ yds.	42 strips, 4½" x 42"	311 squares, 4½" x 4½"
Edge Frames				48 rectangles, 2½" x 4½"
Corner Frames				4 squares, 2½" x 2½"
Window Panes	Scraps	1⅛ yds.	311 squares, 2" x 2"	
Edge Panes			24 squares, 2½" x 2½"	◻
Corner Panes			1 square, 2½" x 2½"	⊠
Backing	Natural Muslin	3¾ yds.		
Binding			6 strips, 3" x 42"	

Quilt Top Assembly

NOTE: *Refer to "Square Frames" (page 7) for general instructions to construct the quilt top.*

1. Following the quilt plan, start in 1 corner of the foundation. Once the first frame is sewn into its 4-square foundation, add the corner frame. Continue adding rows of frames on the diagonal, adding edge frames at the ends of each diagonal row. When you have completed 12 frames on the horizontal outer edge, add the corner frame.

2. Add 2 more diagonal rows. You should now have 14 frames along the vertical outer edge. Add the corner frame.

3. Continue to work diagonally, adding edge frames where indicated. Finish with the remaining corner frame.

4. Refer to "Pressing" on page 13 to press the quilt top.

5. Refer to "Piecing the Backing" on page 15 to piece the backing so it measures approximately 56" x 64".

6. Layer the pieced backing with batting and the quilt top. Referring to "Basting the Quilt" on page 15, pin-baste the window panes to the center of each frame.

7. Referring to "Tacking the Frames" on page 16, tack the frames. Do not tack the frame corners on the edges of the quilt.

8. Referring to "Quilting the Frames and Borders" on page 16, use a blind hem stitch to quilt all of the internal window frames. Do not quilt the corner and edge frames.

9. Stitch the binding strips to the quilt top. Quilt the corner and edge frames. They should just touch the binding and should not overlap. Following the instructions under "Finishing the Quilt" on page 18, bind the edges.

10. Enjoy your quilt.

Foundation and frame grid

Frames

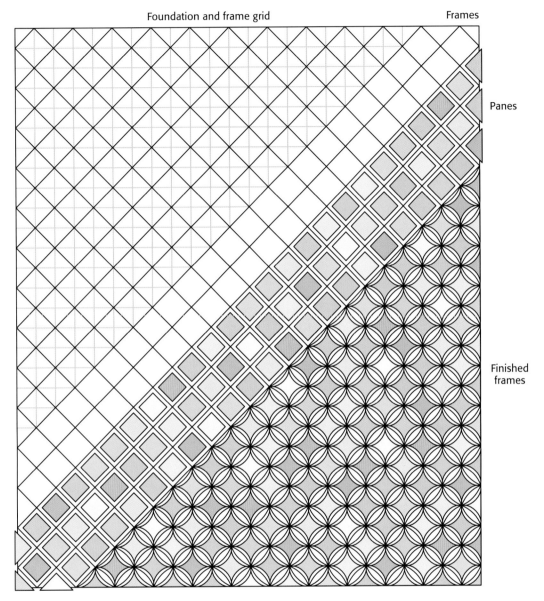

Panes

Finished
frames

Quilt Plan

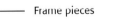 Frame pieces

Foundation pieces

Peaches and Cream

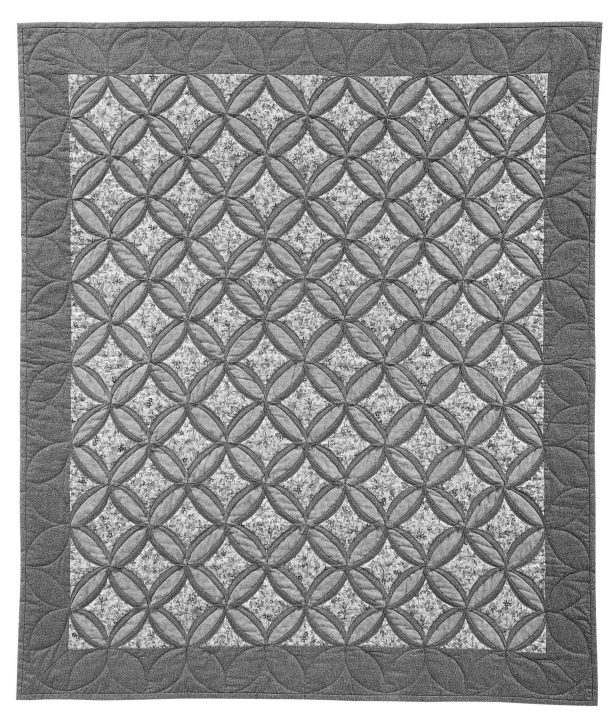

PEACHES AND CREAM, *1998, 43" x 49". Using only three fabrics creates a simple, fresh look.*

Notice how the quilting on the borders reflects the window shape.

MATERIALS: *42"-wide fabric*

Piece	Fabric	Total Yardage Required	First Cut	Second Cut	Third Cut
Foundation	Light Peach	1¾ yds.	16 strips, 3½" x 42"	168 squares, 3½" x 3½"	
Window Frames	Dark Peach	2¾ yds.	14 strips, 6½" x 42"	72 squares, 6½" x 6½"	
Edge Frames				22 rectangles, 3½" x 6½"	
Corner Frames				4 squares, 3½" x 3½"	
Window Panes	Floral Print	¾ yd.	6 strips, 3" x 42"	72 squares, 3" x 3"	
Edge Panes			1 strip, 3½" x 42"	11 squares, 3½" x 3½"	◻
Corner Panes			2 squares, 3" x 3"	◻	
Border	Dark Peach	1½ yds.	2 strips, 4½" x 41", cut on the lengthwise grain		
			2 strips, 4½" x 49", cut on the lengthwise grain		
Binding			4 strips, 3" x 54", cut on the lengthwise grain		
Backing		2¾ yds.			

Quilt Top Assembly

NOTE: *Refer to "Square Frames" (page 7) for general instructions to construct the quilt top.*

1. Following the quilt plan, start in 1 corner of the foundation. Once the first frame is sewn into its 4-square foundation, add the corner frame. Continue adding rows of frames on the diagonal, adding edge frames at the ends of each diagonal row. When you complete 6 frames on the horizontal outer edge, add the corner frame.

2. Add 1 more diagonal row. You should now have 7 frames along the vertical outer edge. Add the corner frame.

3. Continue to work diagonally, adding the edge frames where indicated. Finish with the remaining corner frame.

4. Refer to "Pressing" on page 13 to press the quilt top.

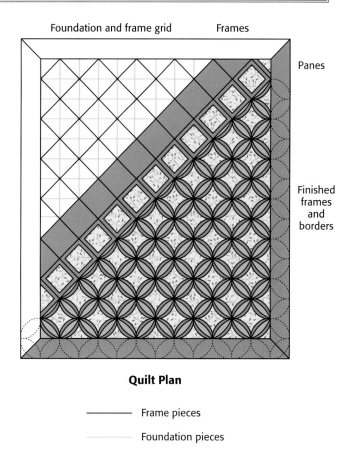

Foundation and frame grid   Frames

Panes

Finished frames and borders

Quilt Plan

——— Frame pieces

——— Foundation pieces

5. Pin the edge and corner window panes in place.

6. Refer to "Mitered Borders" on page 14 to stitch the border strips to the quilt and miter the corners.

7. Refer to "Piecing the Backing" on page 15 to piece the backing so it measures approximately 50" x 56".

8. Layer the pieced backing with batting and the quilt top. Referring to "Basting the Quilt" on page 15, pin-baste the window panes to the center of each frame. Re-pin the edge and corner panes as you come to them. Pin-baste the borders, lining up the border pins with the frame pins.

9. Referring to "Tacking the Frames" on page 16, tack the frames. Do not tack the frame corners that touch the quilt borders.

10. Quilt all of the frames, including the edge and corner frames. Refer to "Quilting the Frames and Borders" on page 16.

11. To make a quilting template for the borders, measure the edge panes from point to point. From paper, make a circle with the diameter

of your measurement. Mine measured approximately 5¾". Select a starting point, then pin the circle to the border so it lines up with 3 points of an edge frame. Machine quilt around the circle in the border, pivoting at each frame point and moving the circle as you go. Sew half circles on the straight part of the border and three-quarter circles on the corners. You should be able to quilt all the way around the border without breaking your thread.

12. Line up the quilting template with the center point of the previously quilted half circle and 2 of the frame points, positioning half the template off the border. Stitch around the template, beginning and ending at the border raw edge. Clip the threads at the ends of each half circle. The pattern that forms should be an extension of the window shape.

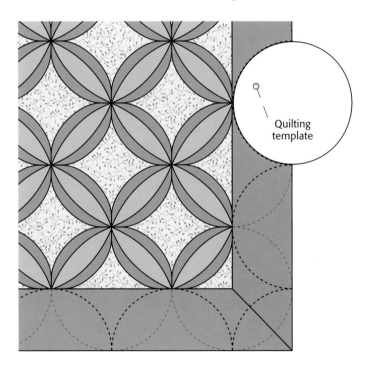

Quilting template

13. Stitch the binding strips to the quilt top and bind the edges, following the instructions under "Finishing the Quilt" on page 18.

14. Enjoy your quilt.

Quilting template

Festive Windows

FESTIVE WINDOWS, *1998, 43" x 43". This quilt, made entirely of batik fabrics,*
was the first quilt I made using the Foundation Grid Method. One background fabric and three frame fabrics
are all that's needed. There are no panes, but you could easily add them for a completely different look.
I also used a buttonhole stitch to quilt the frames and did not tack them.
Feel free to tack them and use another stitch for quilting.

MATERIALS: *42"-wide fabric*

Piece	Fabric	Total Yardage Required	First Cut	Second Cut
Foundation	Multicolored Batik	1¼ yds.	8 strips, 4½" x 42"	64 squares, 4½" x 4½"
Inner Frames	Turquoise Batik	⅝ yd.	1 strip, 8½" x 42"	4 squares, 8½" x 8½"
Inner Border			4 strips, 2½" x 42"	
Middle Frames	Purple Batik	2¼ yds.	3 strips, 8½" x 42"	12 squares, 8½" x 8½"
Outer Border			4 strips, 3½" x 45", cut on the lengthwise grain	
Binding			4 strips, 3" x 45", cut on the lengthwise grain	
Outer Frames	Bright Pink Batik	1⅛ yds.	4 strips, 8½" x 42"	8 squares, 8½" x 8½"
Edge Frames				16 rectangles, 4½ x 8½"
Backing		2¾ yds.		

Quilt Top Assembly

NOTE: *Refer to "Square Frames" (page 7) for general instructions to construct the quilt top.*

1. Following the quilt plan, start in the center, piecing the 4 frames from the turquoise batik. Work around these, adding the 12 frames from the purple batik. The blocks should form a square, 4 frames by 4 frames. On each side, working with the bright pink batik, add 2 square frames; then add an edge frame rectangle to each side of the outer frames. Add 2 edge frame rectangles and a foundation square to finish the corner. Repeat for the remaining 3 sides.

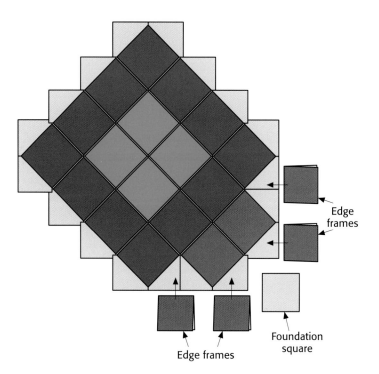

Edge frames

Edge frames

Foundation square

2. Refer to "Pressing" on page 13 to press the quilt top.

3. Stitch the inner and outer border strips together. Refer to "Mitered Borders" on page 14 to stitch the border strips to the quilt and miter the corners.

4. Refer to "Piecing the Backing" on page 15 to piece the backing so it measures approximately 50" x 50".

5. Layer the pieced backing with batting and the quilt top. Referring to "Basting the Quilt" on page 15, pin-baste through the center of each frame.

6. Using a buttonhole stitch, quilt the frames. Refer to "Quilting the Frames and Borders" on page 16. Stitch right up to each point.

7. If desired, tack the frames before quilting and use another stitch for quilting.

8. To quilt the borders, straight stitch ¼" from and parallel to each border seam.

9. Stitch the binding strips to the quilt top and bind the edges, following the instructions under "Finishing the Quilt" on page 18.

10. Enjoy your quilt.

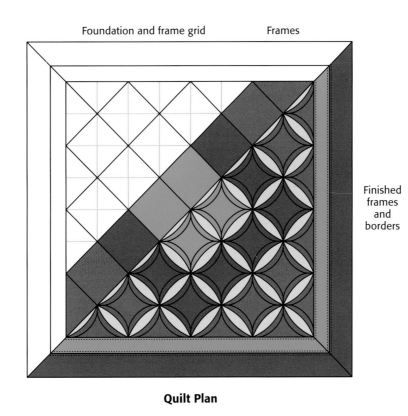

Quilt Plan

——— Frame pieces

——— Foundation pieces

INTRODUCING DIAMONDS AND RECTANGLES

*T*HESE TWO QUILTS show how a diamond emerges when rectangles are used to form the foundation grid. They introduce more complexity to the design but go together almost as easily as the first three quilts.

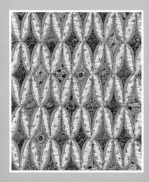

Denim Diamonds

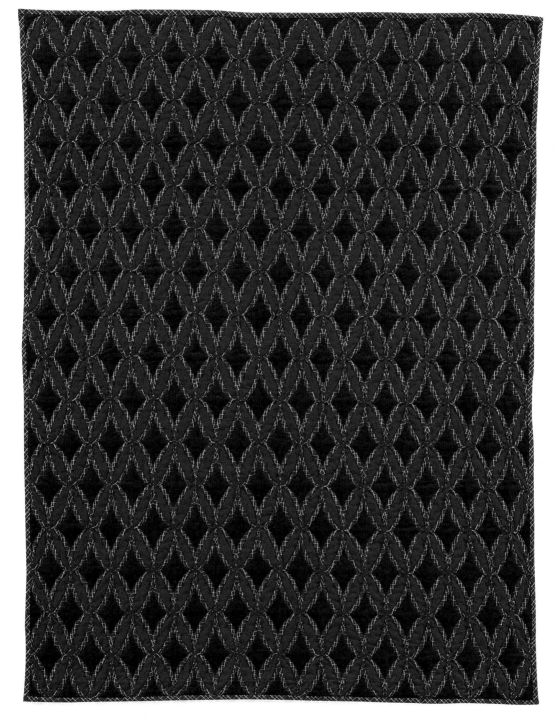

DENIM DIAMONDS, *1999, 49" x 65". Red-and-blue plaid window frames and blue-denim window panes give this quilt a casual, masculine feel. Be sure to select a lightweight denim that's compatible with the other fabrics.*

MATERIALS: *42"-wide fabric*

Piece	Fabric	Total Yardage Required	First Cut	Second Cut
Foundation	Red Tone-on-Tone Print	3¼ yds.	24 strips, 4½" x 42"	384 rectangles, 2½" x 4½"
Window Frames	Red-and-Blue Plaid	8⅛ yds.	12 strips, 21" x 42"	173 Template A
Edge Frames (sides)			3 strips, 4" x 42"	14 Template B
Edge Frames (top and bottom)			3 strips, 6¾" x 42"	22 Template C
Corner Frames				4 Template D
Window Panes	Dark Blue Denim	2⅛ yds.	20 strips, 3" x 42"	173 Template A-WP
Edge Panes (sides)			2 strips, 2" x 42"	14 Template B-WP
Edge Panes (top and bottom)			2 strips, 3¾" x 42"	22 Template C-WP
Corner Panes				2 Template D-WP
				2 Template D-WPr
Backing		3¼ yds.		
Binding	Red-and-Blue Plaid	¾ yd.	235" pieced from 3"-wide bias strips	

Quilt Top Assembly

NOTE: *Refer to "Diamond and Combination Frames" (page 11) for general instructions to construct the quilt top.*

1. Following the quilt plan, start in 1 corner of the foundation. Once the first frame is sewn into the 4 foundation pieces, add the corner frame. Continue adding rows of frames on the diagonal, adding edge frames at the ends of each diagonal row. When you have completed 8 frames on the vertical outer edge, add the corner frame.

2. Add 4 more diagonal rows. You should now have 12 frames along the horizontal outer edge. Add the corner frame.

3. Continue to work diagonally, adding the edge frames where indicated. Finish with the remaining corner frame.

4. Refer to "Pressing" on page 13 to press the quilt top.

5. Refer to "Piecing the Backing" on page 15 to piece the backing so it measures approximately 56" x 72".

6. Layer the pieced backing with batting and the quilt top. Referring to "Basting the Quilt" on page 15, pin-baste the window panes to the center of each frame.

7. Referring to "Tacking the Frames" on page 16, tack the frames. Do not tack the frame corners on the edges of the quilt.

8. Referring to "Quilting the Frames and Borders" on page 16, use a straight stitch to quilt all of the internal window frames. Do not quilt the corner and edge frames.

9. Stitch the binding strips to the quilt top. Quilt the frames on the edges of the quilt. They should just touch the binding and not overlap. Following the instructions under "Finishing the Quilt" on page 18, bind the edges.

10. Enjoy your quilt.

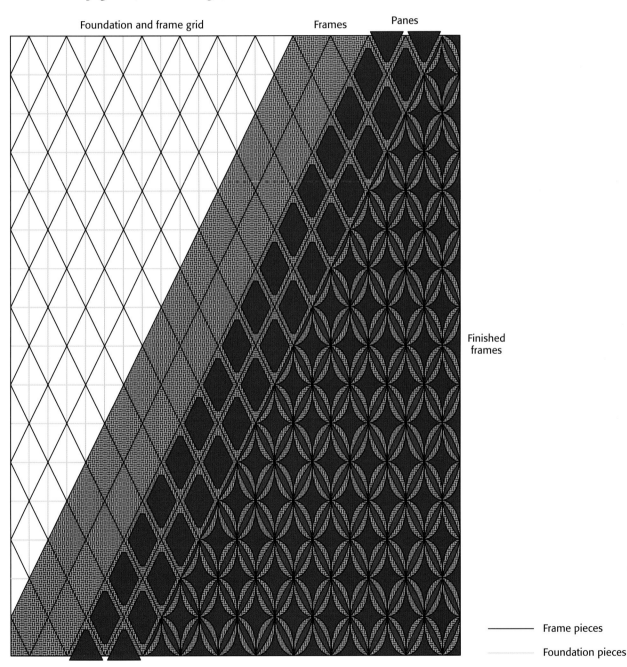

Quilt Plan

Gothic Windows

GOTHIC WINDOWS, *1998, 37" x 50". The diamond frames in this quilt are based on a foundation grid using*
a longer rectangle. This makes the points of the frames a little tricky because they are so deep.
Use sixteen reproduction prints for the panes and you'll find it gives the quilt a vintage look.

MATERIALS: *42"-wide fabric*

Piece	Fabric	Total Yardage Required	First Cut	Second Cut
Foundation	Light Beige Print	1½ yds.	10 strips, 5" x 42"	200 rectangles, 2" x 5"
Window Frames	Medium Tan Print	3⅞ yds.	5 strips, 22" x 42" 1 strip, 6¼" x 42"	85 Template J 1 Template J
Corner Frames				4 Template M
Edge Frames (sides)			2 strips, 3¼" x 42"	8 Template K
Edge Frames (top and bottom)			2 strips, 6¼" x 42"	18 Template L
Panes	16 Assorted Reproduction Prints	⅛ yd. each	16 strips, 2½" x 42" (1 strip from each fabric)	See step 1.
Borders	Dark Brown Print	1½ yds.	2 strips, 4½" x 34", cut on lengthwise grain	
			2 strips, 4½" x 49", cut on lengthwise grain	
Binding			4 strips, 3" x 54", cut on lengthwise grain	
Backing		1½ yds.		

Quilt Top Assembly

NOTE: *Refer to "Diamond and Combination Frames" (page 11) for general instructions to construct the quilt top.*

1. For the window panes, cut 5 Template J-WP and 1 Template L-WP from *each* of the 2½" x 42" strips. From 8 strips, cut 1 Template K-WP. From the remaining fabrics, cut 2 Template L-WP, 2 Template M-WP, and 2 Template M-WPr.

2. Following the quilt plan, start in 1 corner of the foundation to construct the quilt. Once the first frame is sewn into the 4 foundation pieces, add the corner frame. Continue adding rows of frames on the diagonal, adding edge frames at the ends of each diagonal row. When you have completed 5 frames on a vertical edge, add the corner frame.

3. Add 4 more diagonal rows. You should now have 10 frames along the horizontal edge. Add the corner frame.

4. Continue to work diagonally, adding the edge frames where indicated. Finish with the remaining corner frame.

5. Refer to "Pressing" on page 13 to press the quilt top.

6. Pin the edge and corner panes in place.

7. Refer to "Log Cabin Borders" on page 14 to stitch border strips to the quilt.

8. Refer to "Piecing the Backing" on page 15 to piece the backing so it measures approximately 42" x 54".

9. Layer the pieced backing with batting and the quilt top. Referring to "Basting the Quilt" on page 15, pin-baste the window panes to the center of each frame. Re-pin the edge and corner panes as you come to them. Pin-baste the borders, lining up the border pins with the frame pins.

10. Referring to "Tacking the Frames" on page 16, tack the frames. Do not tack the frame corners that touch the quilt borders.

11. Referring to "Quilting the Frames and Borders" on page 16, use a straight stitch to quilt all the frames, including the edge and corner frames.

12. To quilt the borders, straight stitch ¼" from and parallel to each border seam.

13. Stitch the binding strips to the quilt top and bind the edges, following the instructions under "Finishing the Quilt" on page 18.

14. Enjoy your quilt.

Foundation and frame grid   Frames   Panes

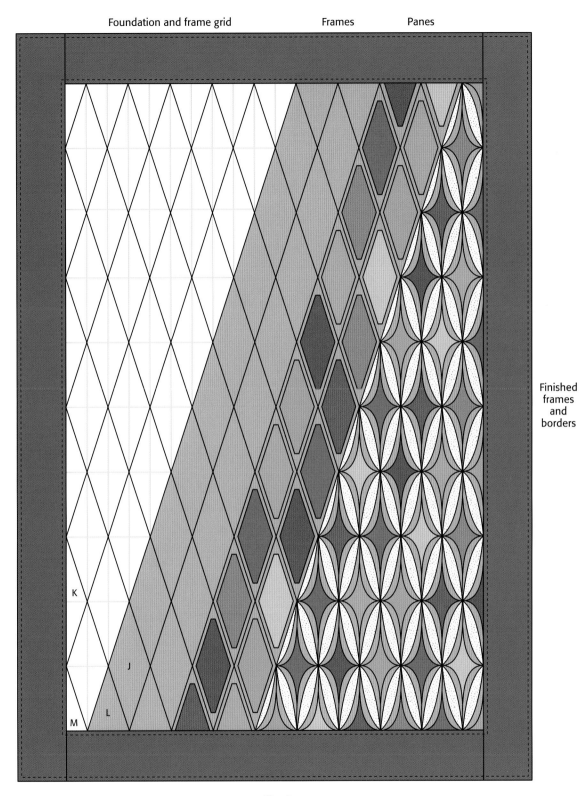

Finished
frames
and
borders

Quilt Plan

———— Frame pieces

———— Foundation pieces

COMBINING SHAPES
AND CREATING
NEW ONES

*W*HEN SQUARES AND rectangles are combined in the foundation grid, some interesting shapes emerge. Although the quilts in this section may appear much more complex and advanced, don't be fooled. Approach these quilts in an organized fashion, and you'll find that they are not as difficult as they look.

Mystical Windows

MYSTICAL WINDOWS, *1999, 49" x 65". The foundation grid for this quilt is based on 2"-wide vertical rows. The horizontal rows change from squares to rectangles to squares. The frames repeat in rows of squares, diamonds, and kites. Notice that whenever a row of foundation squares meets a row of foundation rectangles, a kite frame is used. These shape combinations, along with batik fabrics in bold colors, create a mystical feeling.*

MATERIALS: *42"-wide fabric*

Piece	Fabric	Total Yardage Required	First Cut	Second Cut	Third Cut
Foundation	Turquoise Batik	2½ yds.	14 strips, 2½" x 42"	224 squares, 2½" x 2½"	
			10 strips, 4½" x 42"	160 rectangles, 2½" x 4½"	
	Purple Batik	1⅛ yds.	10 strips, 2½" x 42"	160 squares, 2½" x 2½"	
			2 strips, 4½" x 42"	32 rectangles, 2½" x 4½"	
Frames	Dark Purple Print	3¼ yds.	1 strip, 21" x 42"	12 Template A	
			5 strips, 7¼" x 42"	32 Template E	
			9 strips, 4½" x 42"	68 squares, 4½" x 4½"	
			1 strip, 4" x 42"	6 Template B	
			2 strips, 4½" x 42"	24 rectangles, 2½" x 4½"	
	Dark Turquoise Print	4¼ yds.	2 strips, 21" x 42"	30 Template A	
			1 strip, 7¼" x 42"	2 Template A	
				1 Template E	
			9 strips, 7¼" x 42"	63 Template E	
			7 strips, 4½" x 42"	56 squares, 4½" x 4½"	
			1 strip, 4½" x 42"	16 rectangles, 2½" x 4½"	
Panes	Black-and-Purple Batik	1 yd.	2 strips, 3" x 42"	12 Template A-WP	
			3 strips, 3⅜" x 42"	32 Template E-WP	
			4 strips, 2" x 42"	68 squares, 2" x 2"	
			1 strip, 2" x 42"	8 Template B-WP	
			1 strip, 2¾" x 42"	12 squares, 2¾" x 2¾"	◻
	Turquoise-and-Purple Batik	1¼ yds.	4 strips, 2¾" x 42"	34 Template A-WP	
			3 strips, 2" x 42"	56 squares, 2" x 2"	
			6 strips, 3⅜" x 42"	64 Template E-WP	
			1 strip, 2¾" x 42"	8 squares, 2¾" x 2¾"	◻
Backing		3¼ yds.			
Binding	Black-and-Purple Print	¾ yd.	236", pieced from 3"-wide strips		

Quilt Top Assembly

NOTE: *Refer to "Diamond and Combination Frames" (page 11) for general instructions to construct the quilt top.*

1. Following the quilt plan closely, start with the internal frame square in the lower left corner of the quilt. Add a kite frame. Construct the corner using two 2½" x 4½" rectangles. Continue adding rows on the diagonal, being careful to add the right shape foundation and frame pieces. Add edge frames to the ends of each row.

2. Refer to "Pressing" on page 13 to press the quilt top.

3. Refer to "Piecing the Backing" on page 15 to piece the backing so it measures approximately 56" x 72".

4. Layer the pieced backing with batting and the quilt top. Referring to "Basting the Quilt" on page 15 and the pane layout on page 42, pin-baste the window panes to the center of each frame.

5. Referring to "Tacking the Frames" on page 16, tack the frames. Do not tack the frame corners on the edges of the quilt.

Foundation and frame grid

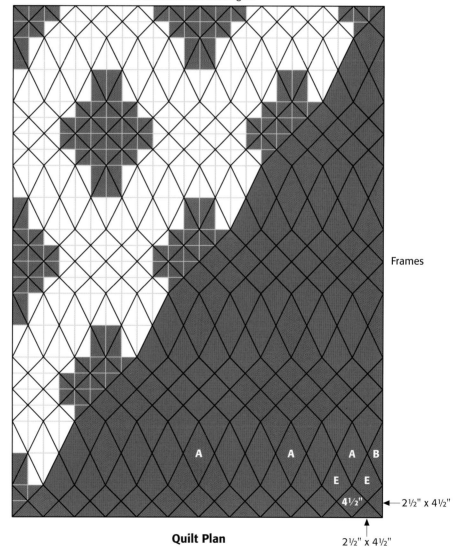

Frames

———— Frame pieces

———— Foundation pieces

Quilt Plan

2½" x 4½"

6. Quilt all of the internal window frames, referring to "Quilting the Frames and Borders" on page 16. Do not quilt the corner and edge frames.

7. Stitch the binding strips to the quilt top. Quilt the frames on the edge of the quilt. They should just touch the binding and not overlap. Following the instructions under "Finishing the Quilt" on page 18, bind the edges.

8. Enjoy your quilt.

Pane layout

Finished frames

Starry Night

STARRY NIGHT, *1998, 45" x 45". The metallic sparkle and the dark blue fabrics were the perfect choice to represent the night sky. In this quilt, the foundation grid uses two sizes of squares with a rectangle and repeats both horizontally and vertically. The trapezoid frame makes its first appearance here and is used along with kite and square frames.*

MATERIALS: *42"-wide fabric*

Piece	Fabric	Total Yardage Required	First Cut	Second Cut
Foundation	Dark Blue Metallic	⅞ yd.	5 strips, 4½" x 42"	36 squares, 4½" x 4½"
			2 strips, 2½" x 42"	20 squares, 2½" x 2½"
	Dark Blue Print	1½ yds.	5 strips, 2½" x 42"	80 squares, 2½" x 2½"
			8 strips, 4½" x 42"	120 rectangles, 2½" x 4½"
Frames	Dark Blue Metallic	2⅛ yds.	8 strips, 7¼" x 42"	52 Template E
			2 strips, 4½" x 42"	12 squares, 4½" x 4½"
			1 strip, 6¾" x 42"	8 Template C
	Dark Blue Print	3 yds.	10 strips, 8" x 42"	48 Template G
			5 strips, 4½" x 42"	12 Template H
				12 Template Hr
Panes	Light Blue Metallic	⅝ yd.	4 strips, 3⅜" x 42"	52 Template E-WP
			1 strip, 2" x 42"	12 squares, 2" x 2"
			1 strip, 3¾" x 42"	8 Template C-WP
	2 Medium Dark Blue Prints	½ yd. each	5 strips, 3½" x 42"	48 Template G-WP
			4 strips, 3¾" x 42"	12 Template H-WP
				12 Template H-WPr
Backing		2¾ yds.		
Binding	Dark Blue Metallic	½ yd.	5 strips, 3" x 42"	

Quilt Top Assembly

NOTE: *Refer to "Diamond and Combination Frames" (page 11) for general instructions to construct the quilt top.*

1. Following the quilt plan closely, start in one corner of the foundation. Once the first frame is sewn into its 4 foundation pieces, add the corner piece. Continue adding rows of frames on the diagonal, adding edge frames as you go.

2. Refer to "Pressing" on page 13 to press the quilt top.

3. Refer to "Piecing the Backing" on page 15 to piece the backing so it measures approximately 50" x 50".

4. Layer the pieced backing with batting and the quilt top. Referring to "Basting the Quilt" on page 15 and the pane layout on page 45, pin-baste the window panes to the center of each frame.

5. Referring to "Tacking the Frames" on page 16, tack the frames. Do not tack the frame corners on the edges of the quilt.

6. Quilt all of the internal frames, referring to "Quilting the Frames and Borders" on page 16. Do not quilt the corner and edge frames.

7. Stitch the binding strips to the quilt top. Quilt the frames on the edge of the quilt. They should just touch the binding and not overlap.

Following the instructions under "Finishing the Quilt" on page 18, bind the edges.

8. Enjoy your quilt.

Foundation and frame grid

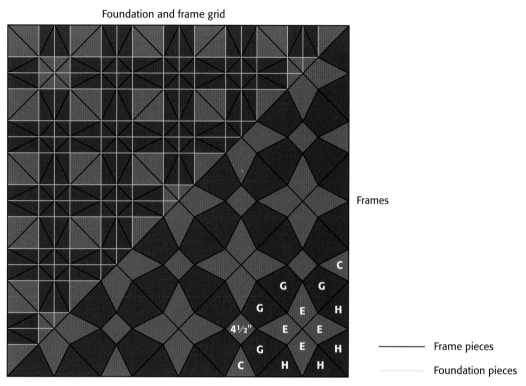

Frames

4½"

C

G   G

G   E   H

E   E

G   E   H

C   H   H

——————— Frame pieces

.... Foundation pieces

Quilt Plan

Pane layout

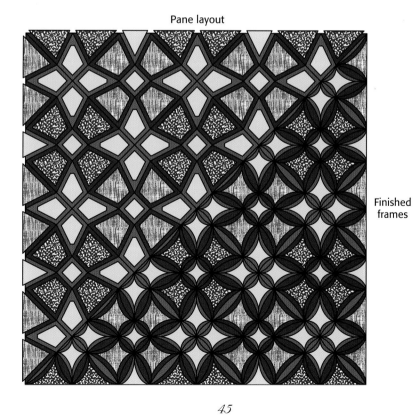

Finished frames

Cathedral Heart

CATHEDRAL HEART, *1999, 39" x 39". Border designed and hand quilted by Wendy Miller. This quilt is a little like a puzzle. The grid does not repeat except to mirror from one side to the other. All the frame shapes are used for this one, including a new one: the large kite. I love hearts, so I just had to include one in this series.*

MATERIALS: *42"-wide fabric*

Piece	Fabric	Total Yardage Required	First Cut	Second Cut	Third Cut
Foundation	Medium Red Star Print	1⅛ yds.	7 strips, 2½" x 42"	108 squares, 2½" x 2½"	
			3 strips, 4½" x 42"	44 rectangles, 2½" x 4½"	
			1 strip, 4½" x 42"	6 squares, 4½" x 4½"	
	Dark Red Print	¼ yd.	1 strip, 2½" x 42"	12 squares, 2½" x 2½"	
			1 strip, 4½" x 42"	12 rectangles, 2½" x 4½"	
Frames	Dark Red Print	2⅞ yds.	6 strips, 7¼" x 42"	4 Template A	
				33 Template E	
				3 Template F	
				3 Template Fr	
			1 strip, 4" x 42"	2 Template B	
			2 strips, 8" x 42"	8 Template G	
			1 strip, 8⅝" x 42"	2 Template I	
			5 strips, 4½" x 42"	31 squares, 4½" x 4½"	
				17 rectangles, 2½" x 4½"	
				2 squares, 2½" x 2½"	
Panes	Dark Red Floral Print	⅝ yd.	2 strips, 3⅜" x 42"	23 Template E-WP	
			1 strip, 2" x 42"	2 Template B-WP	
				3 Template F-WP	
				3 Template F-WPr	
			1 strip, 3½" x 42"	4 Template G-WP	
			1 strip 2" x 42"	20 squares, 2" x 2"	
			1 strip, 3" x 42"	9 squares, 3" x 3"	
				4 squares, 2" x 2"	
	Light Pink Print	⅜ yd.	1 strip, 3⅜" x 42"	10 Template E-WP	
				2 Template A-WP	
			1 strip, 5" x 42"	2 Template A-WP	
				4 Template G-WP	
				2 Template I-WP	
				7 squares, 2" x 2"	
Borders Binding	Dark Red Print	1 yd.	4 strips, 4½" x 42"		
			4 strips, 3" x 42"		
Backing		2½ yds.			

Quilt Top Assembly

NOTE: *Refer to "Diamond and Combination Frames" (page 11) for general instructions to construct the quilt top.*

1. Following the quilt plan closely, construct the quilt top. Begin where desired.

2. Refer to "Pressing" on page 13 to press the quilt top.

3. Pin the edge and corner window panes in place.

4. Refer to "Mitered Borders" on page 14 to stitch the border strips to the quilt and miter the corners.

5. Layer the backing with batting and the quilt top. Referring to "Basting the Quilt" on page 15 and the pane layout on page 49, pin-baste the window panes to the center of each frame. Re-pin the edge and corner panes as you come to them. Pin-baste the borders, lining up the border pins with the frame pins.

6. Referring to "Tacking the Frames" on page 16, tack the frames. Do not tack the frame corners that touch the quilt borders.

7. Refer to "Quilting the Frames and Borders" on page 16. Use a straight stitch to quilt all the frames, including the edge and corner panes.

8. Quilt the borders, using the border and corner quilting templates on pages 49 and 50 and following the border quilting diagram on the pane layout. Stitch along the outer line, then again ¼" inside the line.

9. Stitch the binding strips to the quilt top and bind the edges, following the instructions under "Finishing the Quilt" on page 18.

10. Enjoy your quilt.

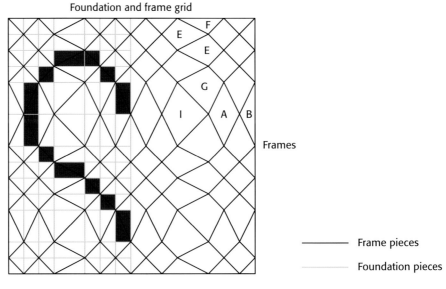

Foundation and frame grid

Frames

———— Frame pieces

———— Foundation pieces

Quilt Plan

Pane layout

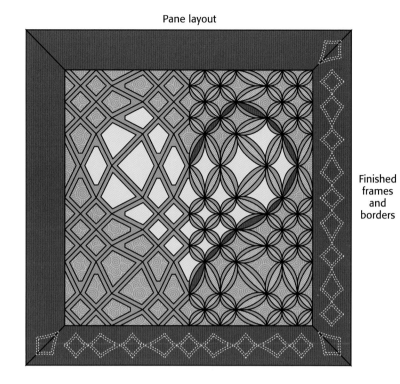

Finished
frames
and
borders

Cathedral Hearts
Corner Quilting Template

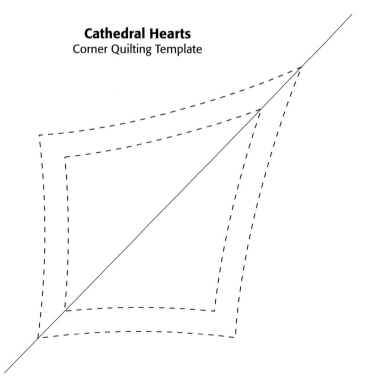

Cathedral Hearts
Border Quilting Templates

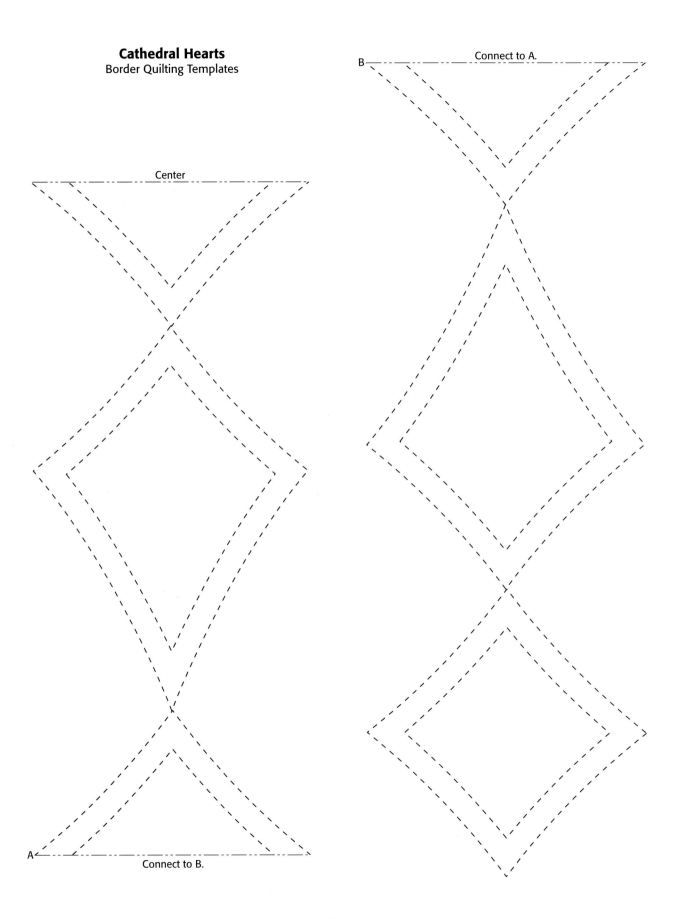

Center

Connect to B.

A

B

Connect to A.

Celestial View

CELESTIAL VIEW, 1999, 49" x 65". The wonderfully complex feel of this quilt demonstrates the versatility of the Foundation Grid Method. By using a combination of square and rectangle foundation pieces along with trapezoid, diamond, kite, and square frames, you'll end up with a wall hanging as intricate and beautiful as a mosaic tile.

MATERIALS: *42"-wide fabric*

Piece	Fabric	Total Yardage Required	First Cut	Second Cut	Third Cut
Foundation	Medium Magenta Solid	2¼ yds.	12 strips, 4½" x 42"	48 squares, 4½" x 4½"	
				96 rectangles, 2½" x 4½"	
			9 strips, 2½" x 42"	144 squares, 2½" x 2½"	
	Dark Blue-Purple	1 yd.	6 strips, 4½" x 42"	96 rectangles, 2½" x 4½"	
			3 strips, 2½" x 42"	48 squares, 2½" x 2½"	
Frames	Medium Magenta Print	4⅝ yds.	3 strips, 21" x 42"	34 Template A	
			10 strips, 8" x 42"	48 Template G	
			3 strips, 6¾" x 42"	28 Template C	
	Medium Magenta Solid	3¼ yds.	7 strips, 7¼" x 42"	48 Template E	
			8 strips, 4½" x 42"	64 squares, 4½" x 4½"	
			2 strips, 8½" x 42"	10 rectangles, 4½" x 8½"	
			1 strip, 8½" x 42"	6 squares, 8½" x 8½"	
Panes	Light Blue-Purple Batik	⅞ yd.	4 strips, 3⅜" x 42"	48 Template E-WP	
			4 strips, 2" x 42"	64 squares, 2" x 2"	
			1 strip, 4¾" x 42"	6 squares, 4¾" x 4¾"	
			1 strip, 5¼" x 42"	6 squares, 5¼" x 5¼"	◺
				2 squares, 2½" x 2½"	◺
	Dark Purple/ Blue/Magenta Print	1⅛ yds.	4 strips, 3" x 42"	34 Template A-WP	
			5 strips, 3½" x 42"	48 Template G-WP	
			2 strips, 3⅜" x 42"	28 Template C-WP	
Backing		3 yds.			
Binding	Dark Blue-Purple	⅝ yd.	6 strips, 3" x 42"		

Quilt Top Assembly

NOTE: *Refer to "Diamond and Combination Frames" (page 11) for general instructions to construct the quilt top.*

1. Following the quilt plan, start in the lower left corner. Once the first frame is sewn into its 4 foundation pieces, add the corner frame. Continue adding rows of frames on the diagonal, adding edge and corner frames where indicated.

2. Refer to "Pressing" on page 13 to press the quilt top.

3. Refer to "Piecing the Backing" on page 15 to piece the backing so it measures approximately 54" x 72".

4. Layer the pieced backing with batting and the quilt top. Referring to "Basting the Quilt" on page 15 and the pane layout on page 54, pin-baste the window panes to the center of each frame.

5. Referring to "Tacking the Frames" on page 16, tack the frames. Do not tack the frame corners on the edges of the quilt.

6. Quilt all of the internal window frames, referring to "Quilting the Frames and Borders" on page 16. Do not quilt the corner and edge frames.

7. Stitch the binding strips to the quilt top. Quilt the frames on the edge of the quilt. They should just touch the binding and not overlap. Follow the instructions under "Finishing the Quilt" on page 18 to bind the edges.

8. Enjoy your quilt.

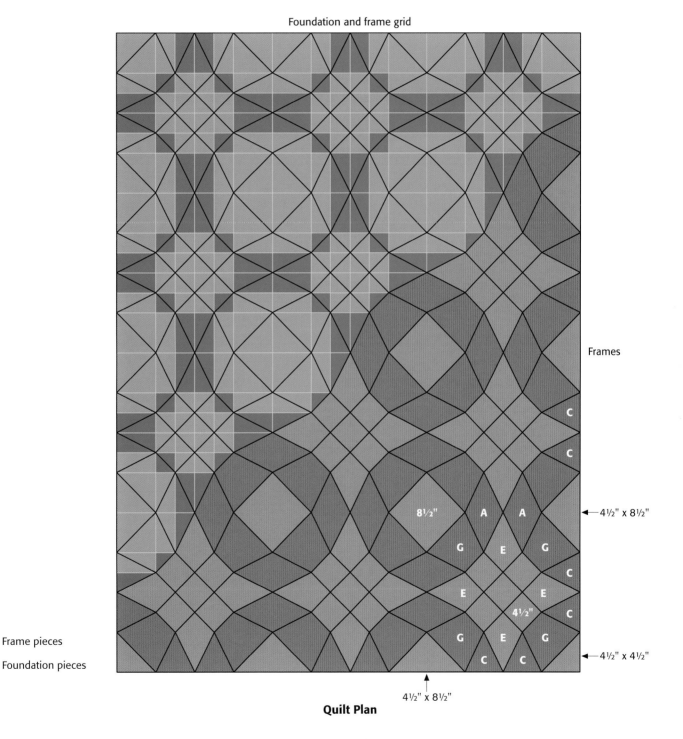

Foundation and frame grid

Frames

8½"

A A

G E G

C

C

4½"

E E

4½"

G E G

C C

4½" x 8½"

C

C

4½" x 8½"

4½" x 4½"

Frame pieces
Foundation pieces

4½" x 8½"

Quilt Plan

Pane layout

Finished
frames

USING AN
ISOMETRIC GRID

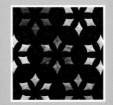

*U*sing an isometric grid to form the foundation of these three quilts only makes them look more complex; it does not mean they are more difficult to construct. Pay close attention to the cutting instructions and layouts provided, and you'll have no trouble venturing into this new territory.

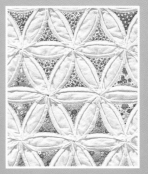

Garden Windows

GARDEN WINDOWS, *1999, 56½" x 64". In this quilt, Cathedral Windows meet Grandmother's Flower Garden.*
The results are pure magic when you use 1940s reproduction fabrics for the window panes. Because this quilt is a little more dif-
ficult, it's important that the triangle frames are cut so that all three sides are on the bias.

MATERIALS: *42"-wide fabric*

Piece	Fabric	Total Yardage Required	First Cut	Second Cut
Foundation	White Tone-on-Tone Print	3¾ yds.	47 strips, 2½" x 42"	742 Template N
				2 Template Q
				2 Template Qr
			3 strips, 1¾" x 42"	26 Template O
			2 strips, 2⅞" x 42"	16 Template P
Frames	White Tone-On-Tone Print	8½ yds.	See step 1.	
Panes	25 Assorted Reproduction Prints	⅛ yd. each	See step 2.	
Backing		3½ yds.		
Binding	White Tone-on-Tone Print	⅞ yd.	246" pieced from 3"-wide bias strips	

Quilt Top Assembly

NOTE: *Refer to "Isometric Grid Frames" (page 12) for general instructions to construct the quilt top.*

1. Refer to "Cutting the Pieces" on page 5 to cut the white tone-on-tone frame fabric off-grain. Cut 64 strips, each 4½" wide. From the strips, cut 486 Template R and 36 Template S frames.

2. Using Template R-WP, cut 18 pieces from *each* of the 25 reproduction prints. Cut 6 additional pieces from *each* of 2 fabrics. Cut 3 additional pieces from *each* of 8 fabrics.

3. From 18 reproduction prints, cut 1 piece using Template S-WP and 1 piece using Template S-WPr.

4. Following the quilt plan, begin with the second row and work in horizontal rows to construct the quilt top. Add edge frames at the ends of each row. When you have completed 17 rows, complete the first row. Add the corners.

NOTE: *On a quilt this large, the top and bottom rows are added last to keep those edges from becoming worn from handling.*

5. Refer to "Pressing" on page 13 to press the quilt top.

6. Refer to "Piecing the Backing" on page 15 to piece the backing so it measures approximately 63" x 71".

7. Layer the pieced backing with batting and the quilt top. Referring to "Basting the Quilt" on page 15 and the pane layout on page 60, pin-baste a window pane to the center of each frame. Pin matching sets of 6 R-WP pieces to the internal frames, as shown in the pane layout. Fill in the upper and lower edges with matching sets of 3 R-WP pieces. Fill in edge panes with 1 each of matching S-WP and S-WPr pieces. Place the remaining pane pieces in each corner.

8. Referring to "Tacking the Frames" on page 16, tack the frames. Do not tack the frame corners on the edges of the quilt.

9. Referring to "Quilting the Frames and Borders" on page 16, quilt all of the internal window frames. Do not quilt the corner and edge frames.

10. Fold the short side of each Template S edge frame over its pane and pin it in place.

11. Stitch the binding strips to the quilt top, stitching only the edge panes into the binding seam. Quilt the edge frames. They should just touch the binding and not overlap. Follow the instructions under "Finishing the Quilt" on page 18 to bind the edges.

12. Enjoy your quilt.

Foundation and frame grid

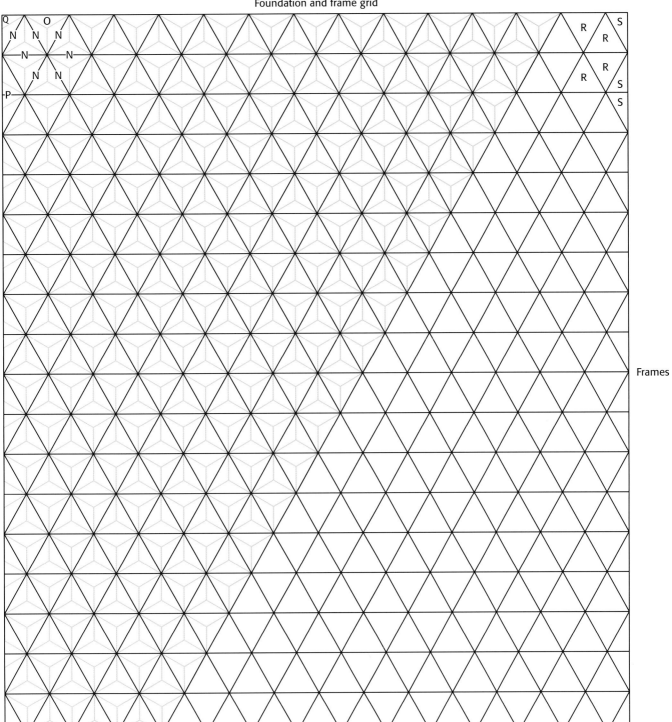

Frames

Quilt Plan

 Frame pieces

Foundation pieces

Pane layout

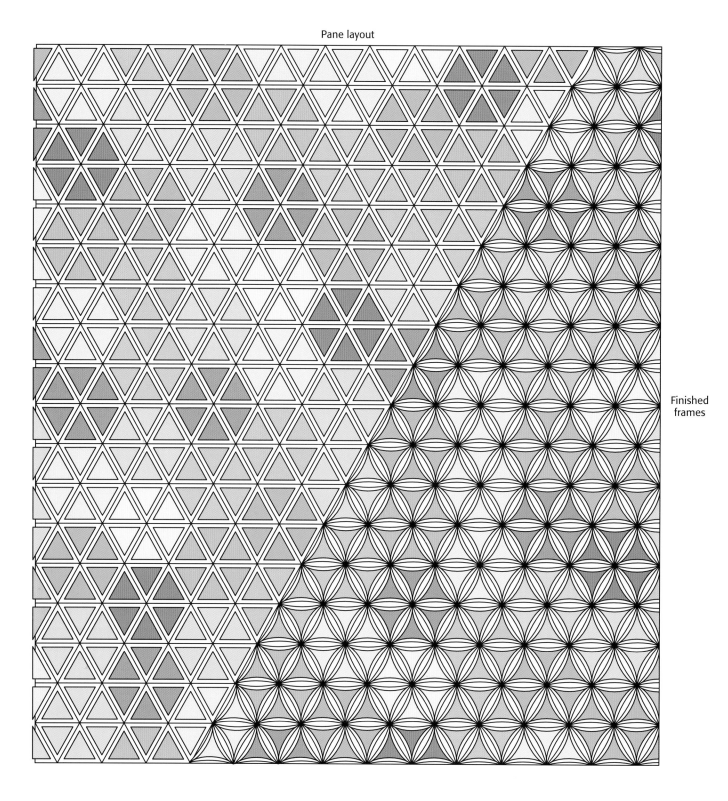

Finished
frames

Tumbling Windows

TUMBLING WINDOWS, *1998, 37" x 41". Tumbling Blocks were the inspiration for these diamond-shaped Cathedral Windows. To achieve the look, three diamond frames are paired with wedge-shaped foundation pieces to visually form a hexagon. When the panes are placed only on the horizontal rows of diamonds, the Tumbling Blocks appear.*

MATERIALS: *42"-wide fabric*

Piece	Fabric	Total Yardage Required	First Cut	Second Cut
Foundation	Off-White Tone-on-Tone Print	1⅜ yds.	11 strips, 3¾" x 42"	115 Template T
			1 strip, 2½" x 42"	8 Template U
			1 strip, 2¾" x 42"	10 Template V
Frames	Green Print	⅞ yd.	3 strips, 7½" x 42"	14 Template W
			1 strip, 4⅛" x 42"	2 Template Y
				2 Template X
	Red Print	⅞ yd.	3 strips, 7½" x 42"	14 Template W
			1 strip, 4⅛" x 42"	2 Template Y
				2 Template X
	Brown Print	⅞ yd.	3 strips, 7½" x 42"	15 Template W
			1 strip, 3¾" x 42"	1 Template X
				2 Template Z
	Blue Print	⅞ yd.	3 strips, 7½" x 42"	15 Template W
			1 strip, 3¾" x 42"	1 Template X
				2 Template Z
Panes	Brown-and-Black Stripe	¼ yd.	2 strips, 3" x 42"	18 Template W-WP
Borders Binding	Brown-and-Black Stripe	1¼ yds.	4 strips, 4½" x 42"	
			146" pieced from 3"-wide strips	
Backing		1 yd.		

Quilt Top Assembly

NOTE: *Refer to "Isometric Grid Frames" (page 12) for general instructions to construct the quilt top.*

1. Following the quilt plan closely, construct the quilt top. Begin where desired. Add the edge and corner frames where indicated.

2. Refer to "Pressing" on page 13 to press the quilt top.

3. Refer to "Mitered Borders" on page 14 to stitch the border strips to the quilt and miter the corners.

4. Layer the backing with batting and the quilt top. Referring to "Basting the Quilt" on page 15 and the pane layout on page 63, pin-baste the window panes on the frames. Pin-baste the borders, lining up the border pins with the frame pins.

5. Referring to "Tacking the Frames" on page 16, tack the frames. Do not tack the frame corners that touch the quilt borders.

6. Referring to "Quilting the Frames and Borders" on page 16, quilt all of the frames, including the edge and corner panes. Follow the border quilting diagram on the pane layout to quilt the borders.

7. Stitch the binding strips to the quilt top and bind the edges, following the instructions under "Finishing the Quilt" on page 18.

8. Enjoy your quilt.

Foundation and frame grid

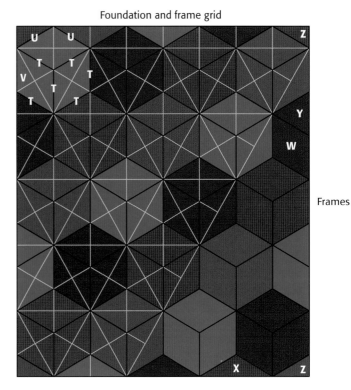

Frames

—————— Frame pieces

—————— Foundation pieces

Quilt Plan

Pane layout

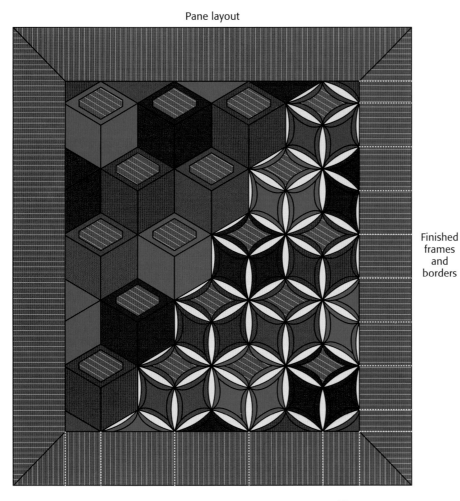

Finished frames and borders

Tumbling Stars

TUMBLING STARS, *1999, 48" x 54". Bright-color batik stars stand out on a background of solid black in this version of* TUMBLING WINDOWS. *A multicolored batik in the border ties them all together.*

MATERIALS: *42"-wide fabric*

Piece	Fabric	Total Yardage Required	First Cut	Second Cut
Foundation	Black Solid	2⅜ yds.	26 strips, 3" x 42"	376 Template AA
			1 strip, 2⅝" x 42"	16 Template BB
Frames	Black Solid	4¼ yds.	9 strips, 14½" x 42"	181 Template CC
			3 strips, 3" x 42"	14 Template DD
			1 strip, 4⅞" x 42"	6 Template EE
			1 strip, 3" x 42"	2 Template FF
				2 Template FFr
Panes	10 Bright-Color Batiks	⅛ yd. each	10 strips, 2" x 42" (1 from each color)	See steps 1 and 2.
Backing	Black Solid	3½ yds.	2 lengths, 42" x 63", cut on the lengthwise grain	
Inner Border			See step 6.	
Middle Border	Multicolored Batik	1¾ yds.	4 strips, 1¼" x 63", cut on the lengthwise grain	
Outer Border	Black Solid	1¾ yds.	4 strips, 4½" x 63", cut on the lengthwise grain	
Binding			4 strips, 3" x 63", cut on the lengthwise grain	

Quilt Top Assembly

NOTE: *Refer to "Isometric Grid Frames" (page 12) for general instructions to construct the quilt top.*

1. From the bright-color batik fabrics, cut 1 Template EE-WP piece from the corner of 6 colors. Cut 1 Template FF-WP *each* from 2 remaining colors. Cut 1 Template FF-WPr *each* from the 2 remaining colors.

2. From each of the 10 colors, cut a 2"-wide strip. Cut 12 Template CC-WP pieces from 8 of the fabrics for the interior stars. Cut an additional 2 CC-WP pieces and 2 DD-WP pieces from 2 of the 8 fabrics. From the remaining 2 fabrics, cut 8 Template CC-WP pieces and 2 Template DD-WP pieces.

3. Following the quilt plan, work in horizontal rows to construct the quilt top. Add edge and corner frames where indicated.

4. Refer to "Pressing" on page 13 to press the quilt top.

5. Follow the pane layout to pin-baste the window panes along the quilt edges.

6. From 1 backing length, cut 4 lengthwise strips, each 1¾" wide.

7. Stitch the 3 border strips together in the order indicated. Refer to "Mitered Borders" on page 14 to stitch the border strips to the quilt and miter the corners.

8. Refer to "Piecing the Backing" on page 15 to piece the backing so it measures approximately 56" x 63".

9. Layer the pieced backing with batting and the quilt top. Referring to "Basting the Quilt" on page 15 and the pane layout on page 67, pin-baste the window panes to the center of each frame. Pin-baste the quilt borders, lining up the pins in the border with the frame pins.

10. Referring to "Tacking the Frames" on page 16, tack the frames. Do not tack the frame corners that touch the borders of the quilt.

11. Quilt all of the frames, including the edge and corner frames. Refer to "Quilting the Frames and Borders" on page 16. Follow the border quilting diagram on the pane layout to quilt the borders.

12. Stitch the binding strips to the quilt top and bind the edges, following the instructions under "Finishing the Quilt" on page 18.

13. Enjoy your quilt.

Foundation and frame grid

Frames

——— Frame pieces

——— Foundation pieces

Quilt Plan

Pane layout

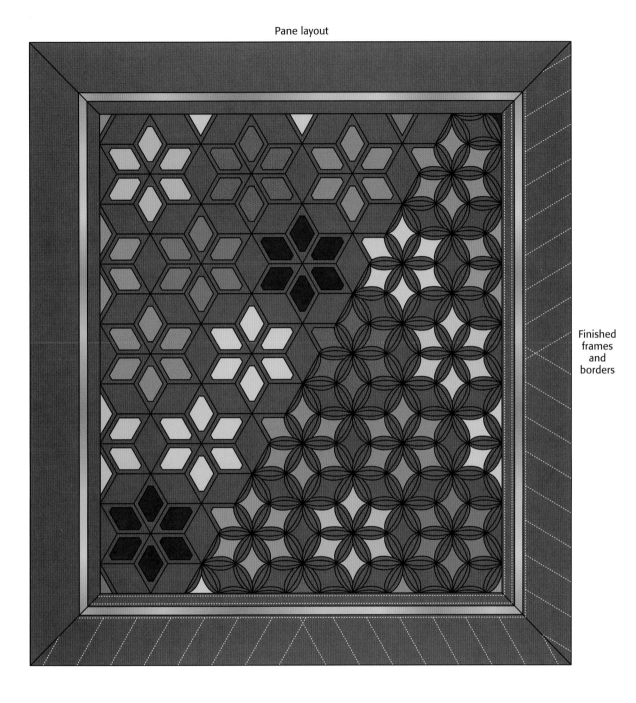

Finished
frames
and
borders

TEMPLATES

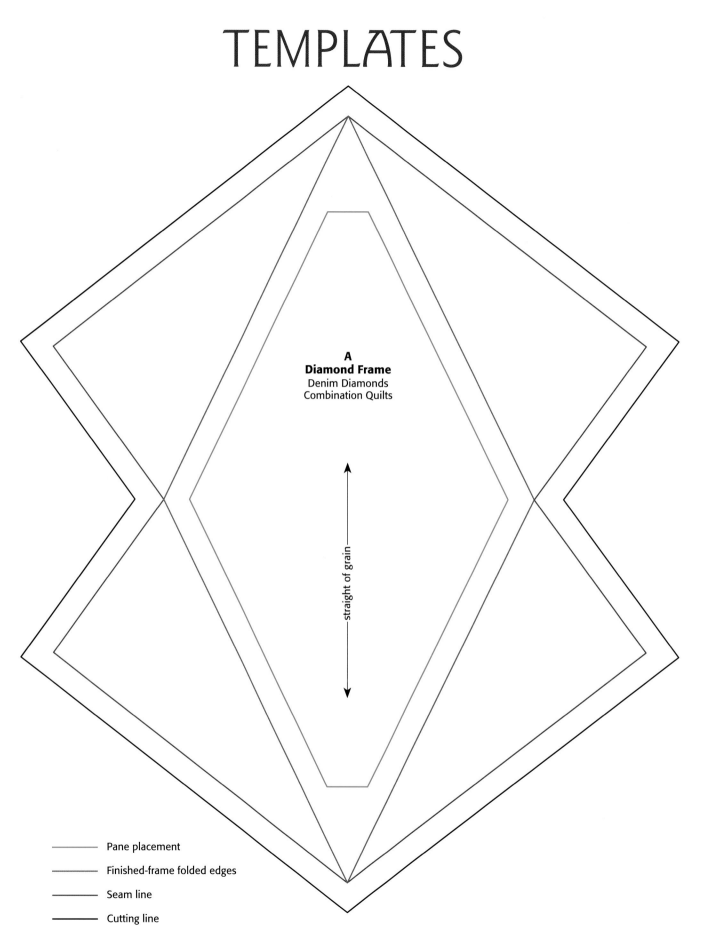

A
Diamond Frame
Denim Diamonds
Combination Quilts

straight of grain

Pane placement

Finished-frame folded edges

Seam line

Cutting line

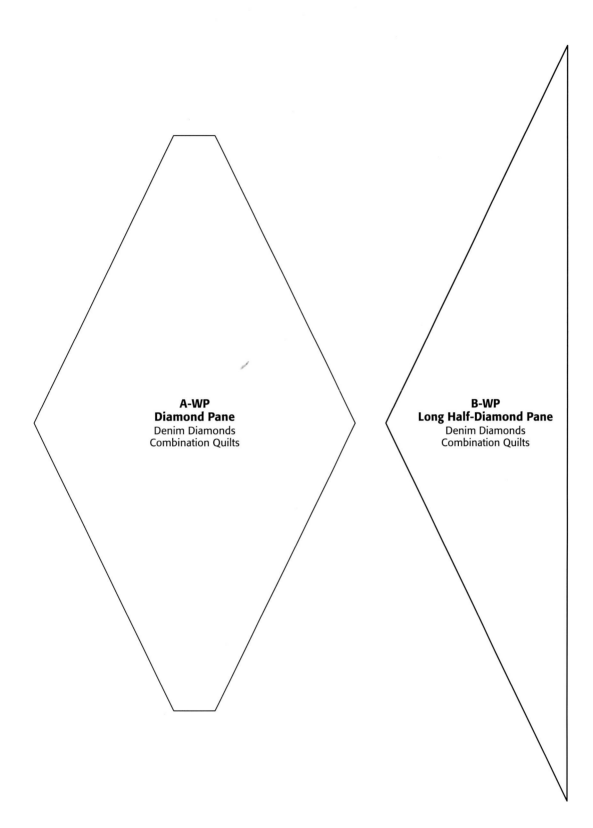

A-WP
Diamond Pane
Denim Diamonds
Combination Quilts

B-WP
Long Half-Diamond Pane
Denim Diamonds
Combination Quilts

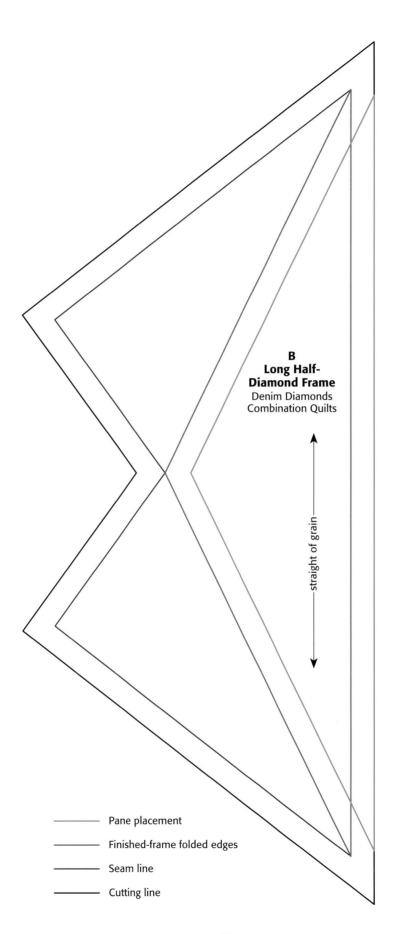

B
Long Half-
Diamond Frame
Denim Diamonds
Combination Quilts

straight of grain

Pane placement

Finished-frame folded edges

Seam line

Cutting line

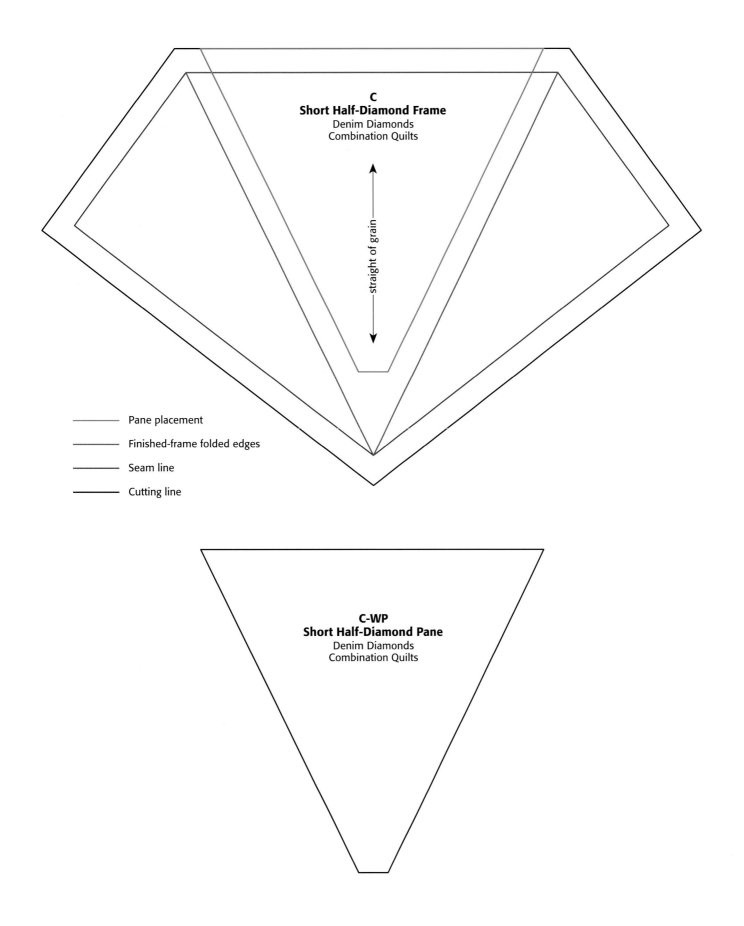

C
Short Half-Diamond Frame
Denim Diamonds
Combination Quilts

straight of grain

Pane placement

Finished-frame folded edges

Seam line

Cutting line

C-WP
Short Half-Diamond Pane
Denim Diamonds
Combination Quilts

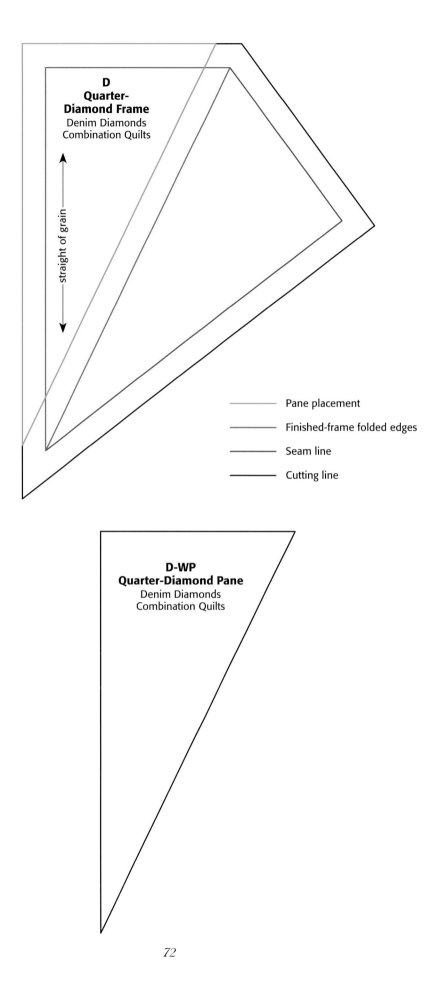

D
Quarter-Diamond Frame
Denim Diamonds
Combination Quilts

straight of grain

Pane placement

Finished-frame folded edges

Seam line

Cutting line

D-WP
Quarter-Diamond Pane
Denim Diamonds
Combination Quilts

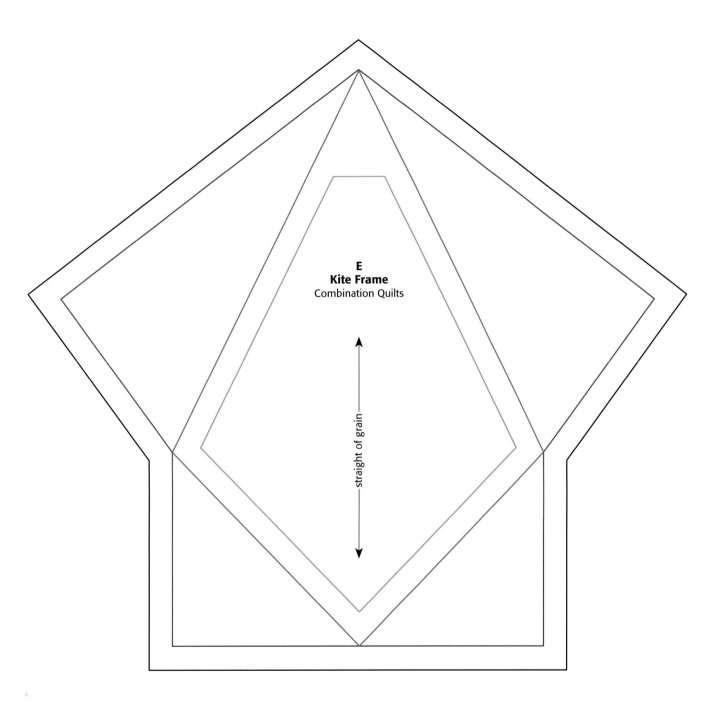

E
Kite Frame
Combination Quilts

straight of grain

Pane placement

Finished-frame folded edges

Seam line

Cutting line

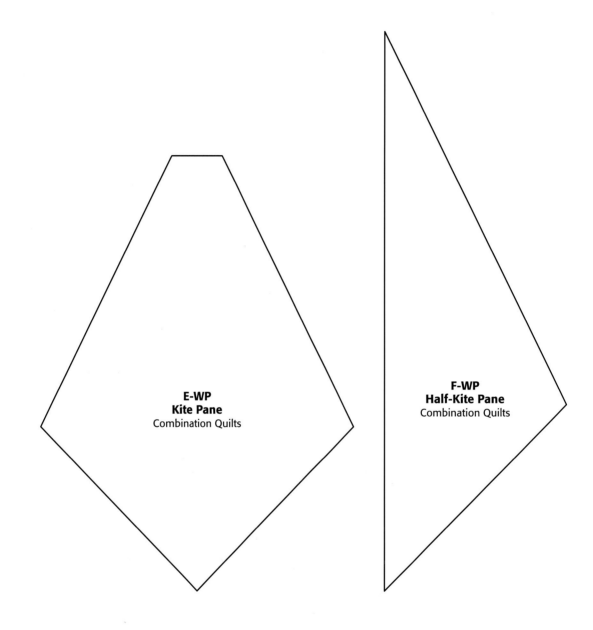

E-WP
Kite Pane
Combination Quilts

F-WP
Half-Kite Pane
Combination Quilts

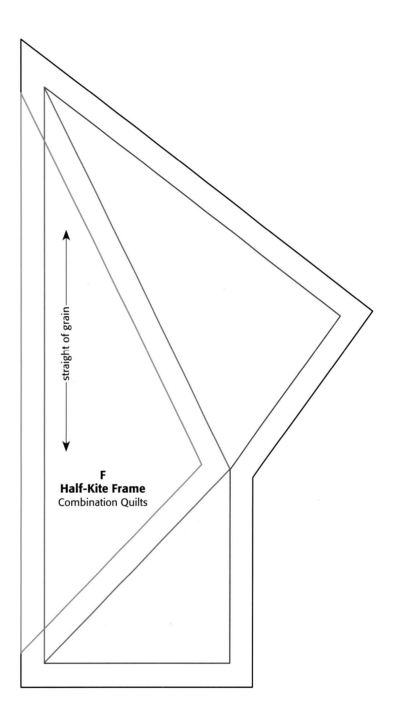

Pane placement

Finished-frame folded edges

Seam line

Cutting line

straight of grain

**F
Half-Kite Frame**
Combination Quilts

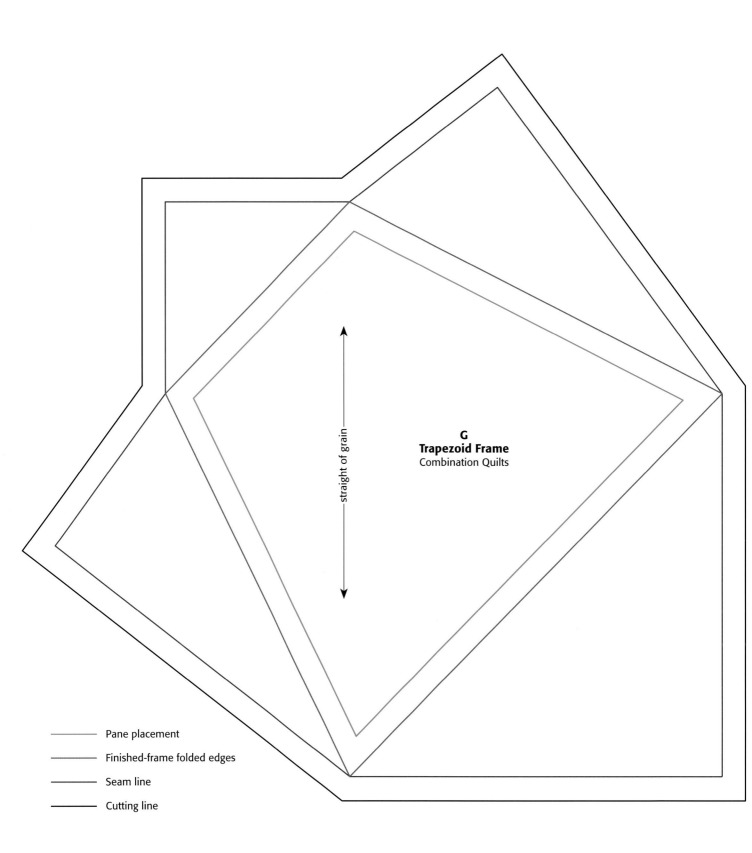

G
Trapezoid Frame
Combination Quilts

straight of grain

Pane placement

Finished-frame folded edges

Seam line

Cutting line

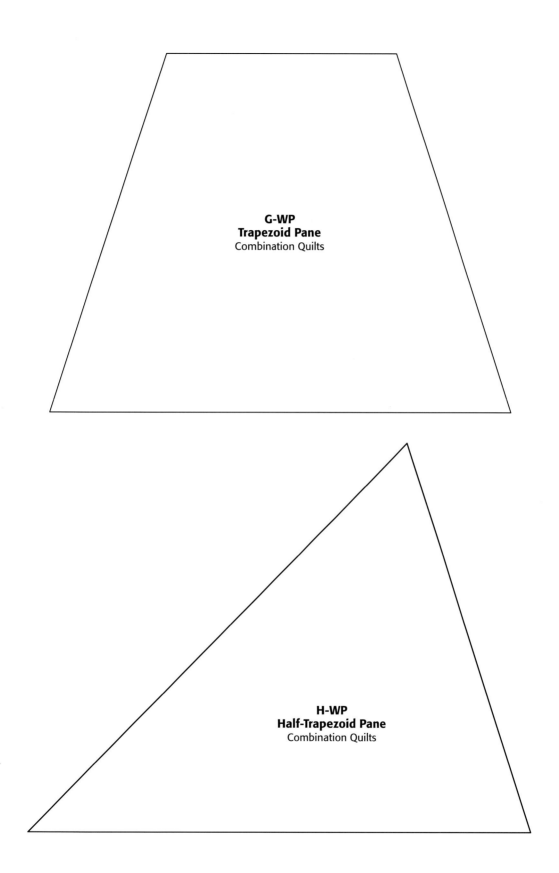

G-WP
Trapezoid Pane
Combination Quilts

H-WP
Half-Trapezoid Pane
Combination Quilts

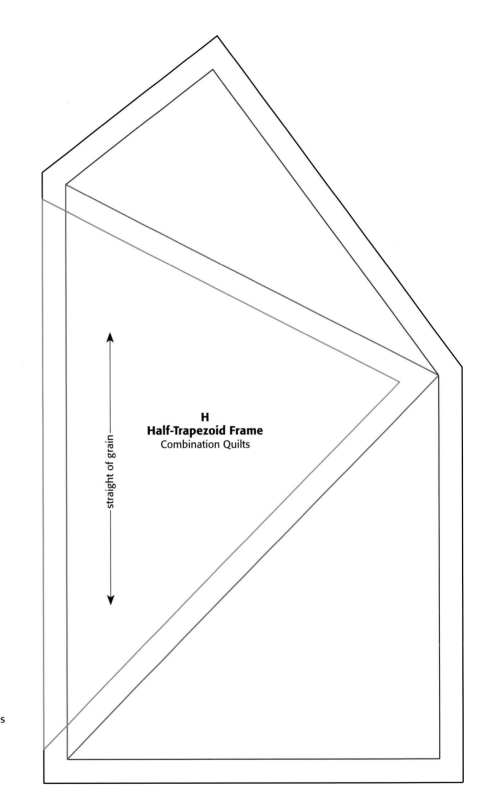

H
Half-Trapezoid Frame
Combination Quilts

straight of grain

Pane placement

Finished-frame folded edges

Seam line

Cutting line

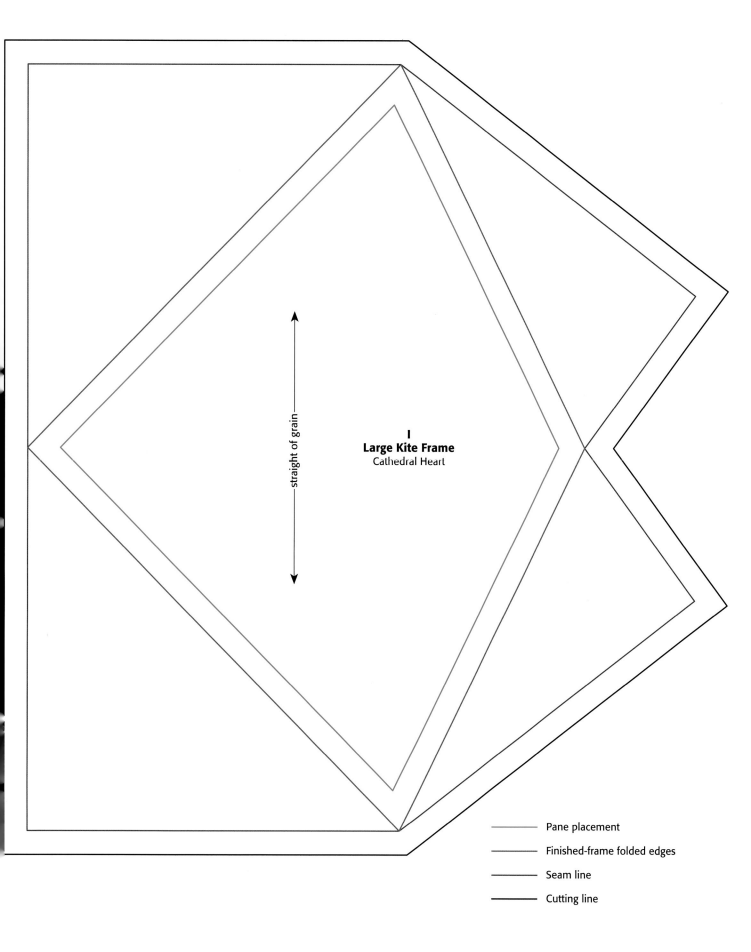

I
Large Kite Frame
Cathedral Heart

straight of grain

Pane placement

Finished-frame folded edges

Seam line

Cutting line

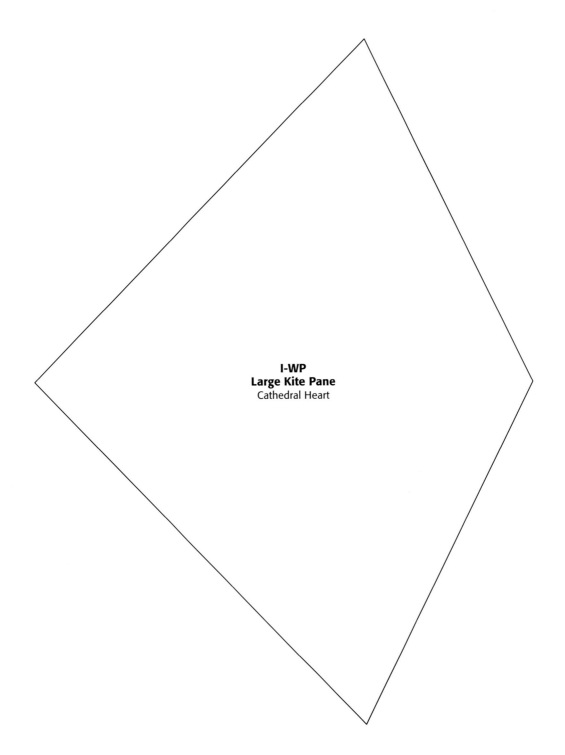

I-WP
Large Kite Pane
Cathedral Heart

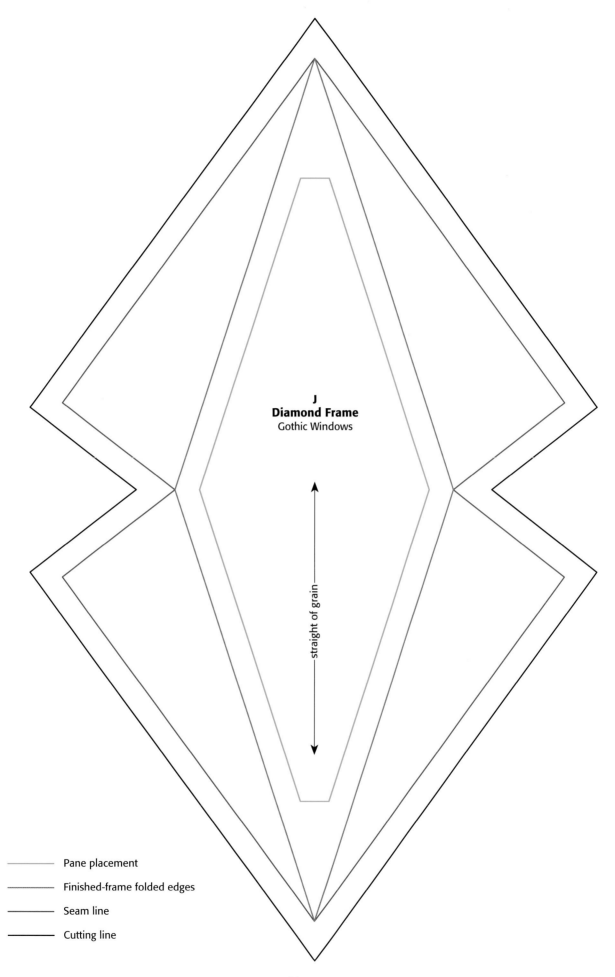

J
Diamond Frame
Gothic Windows

straight of grain

Pane placement

Finished-frame folded edges

Seam line

Cutting line

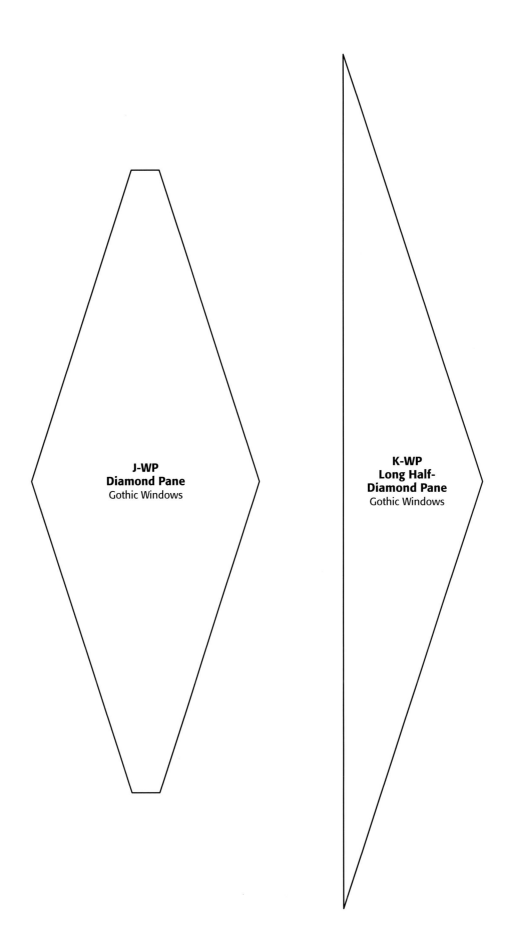

J-WP
Diamond Pane
Gothic Windows

K-WP
Long Half-
Diamond Pane
Gothic Windows

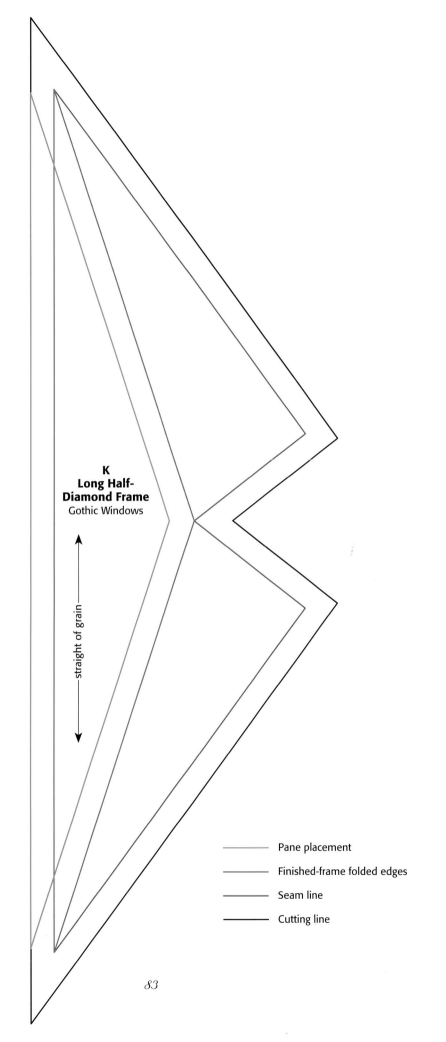

K
Long Half-
Diamond Frame
Gothic Windows

straight of grain

Pane placement

Finished-frame folded edges

Seam line

Cutting line

83

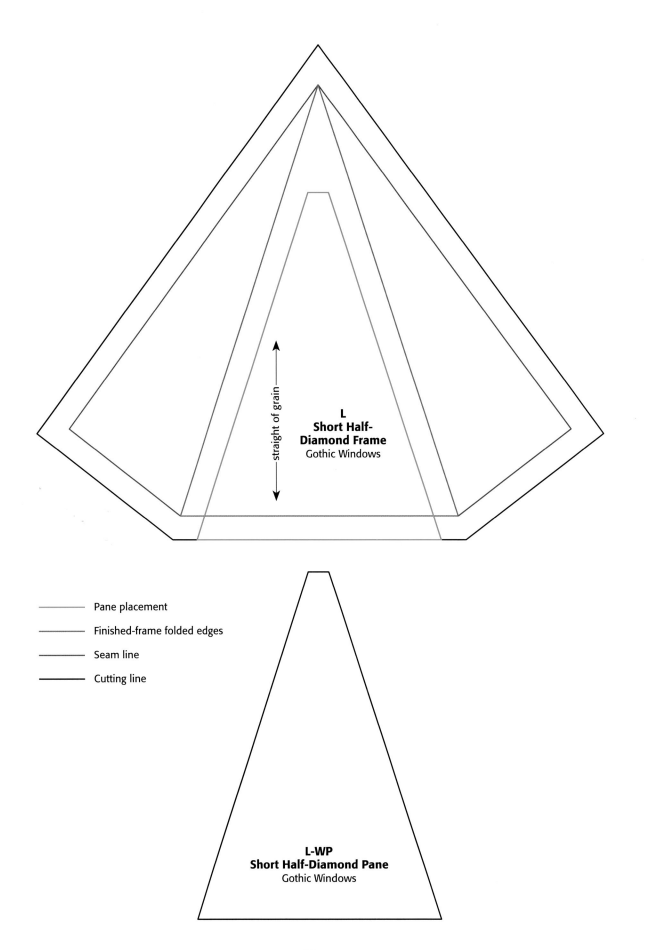

straight of grain

L
Short Half-
Diamond Frame
Gothic Windows

Pane placement

Finished-frame folded edges

Seam line

Cutting line

L-WP
Short Half-Diamond Pane
Gothic Windows

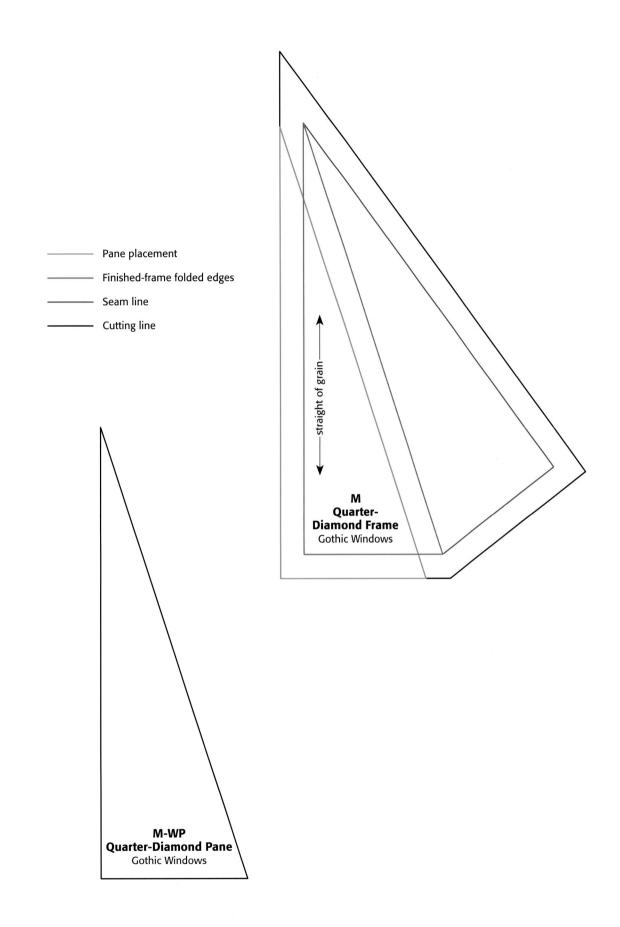

Pane placement

Finished-frame folded edges

Seam line

Cutting line

straight of grain

**M
Quarter-
Diamond Frame**
Gothic Windows

**M-WP
Quarter-Diamond Pane**
Gothic Windows

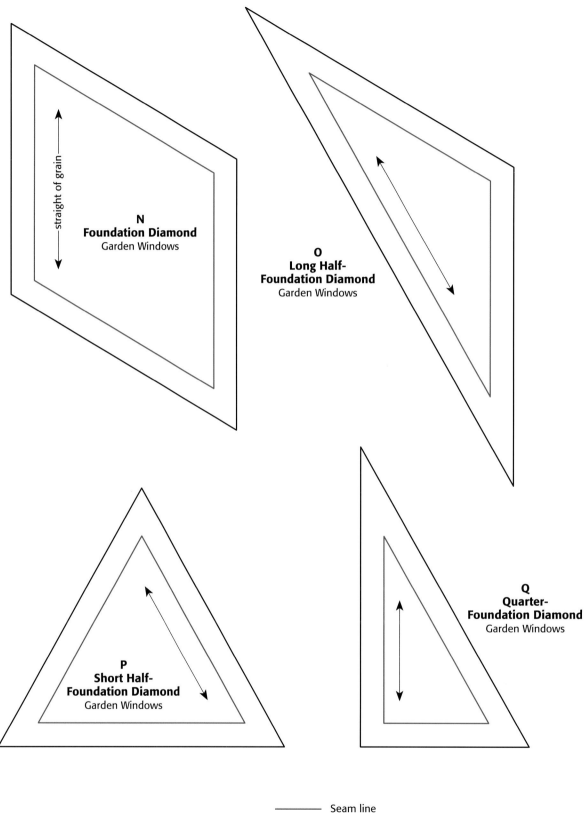

N
Foundation Diamond
Garden Windows

straight of grain

O
Long Half-
Foundation Diamond
Garden Windows

P
Short Half-
Foundation Diamond
Garden Windows

Q
Quarter-
Foundation Diamond
Garden Windows

———— Seam line

———— Cutting line

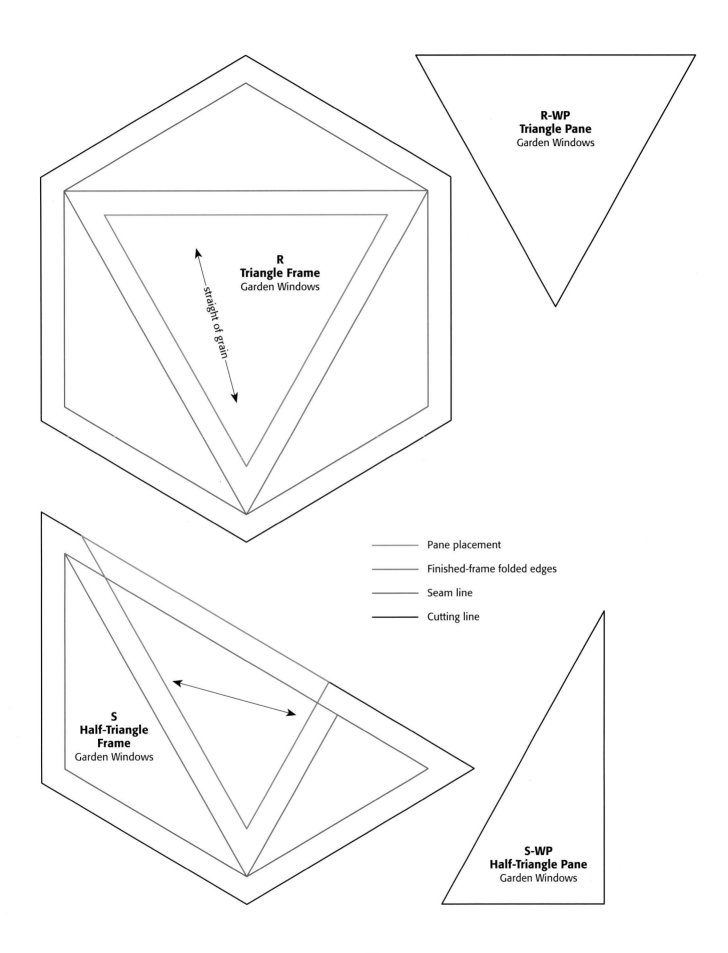

R-WP
Triangle Pane
Garden Windows

R
Triangle Frame
Garden Windows

straight of grain

Pane placement

Finished-frame folded edges

Seam line

Cutting line

S
Half-Triangle
Frame
Garden Windows

S-WP
Half-Triangle Pane
Garden Windows

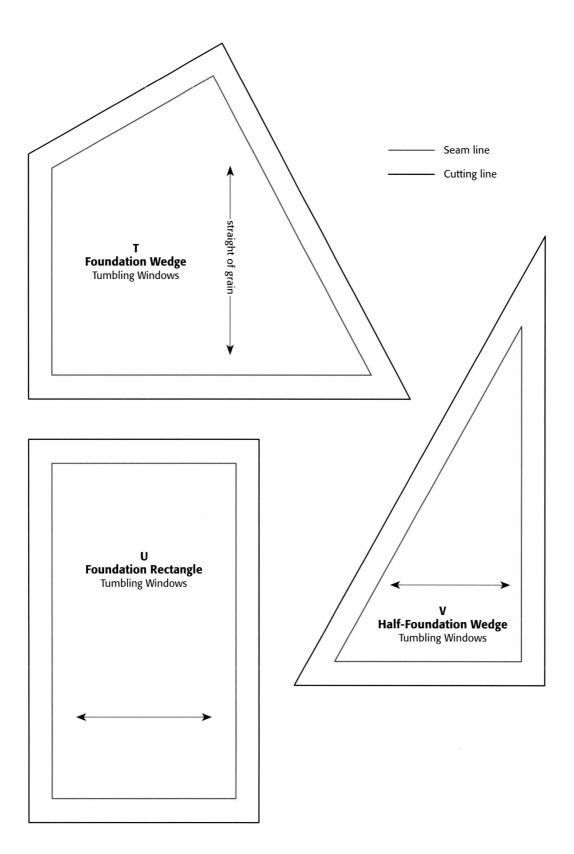

Seam line

Cutting line

T
Foundation Wedge
Tumbling Windows

straight of grain

U
Foundation Rectangle
Tumbling Windows

V
Half-Foundation Wedge
Tumbling Windows

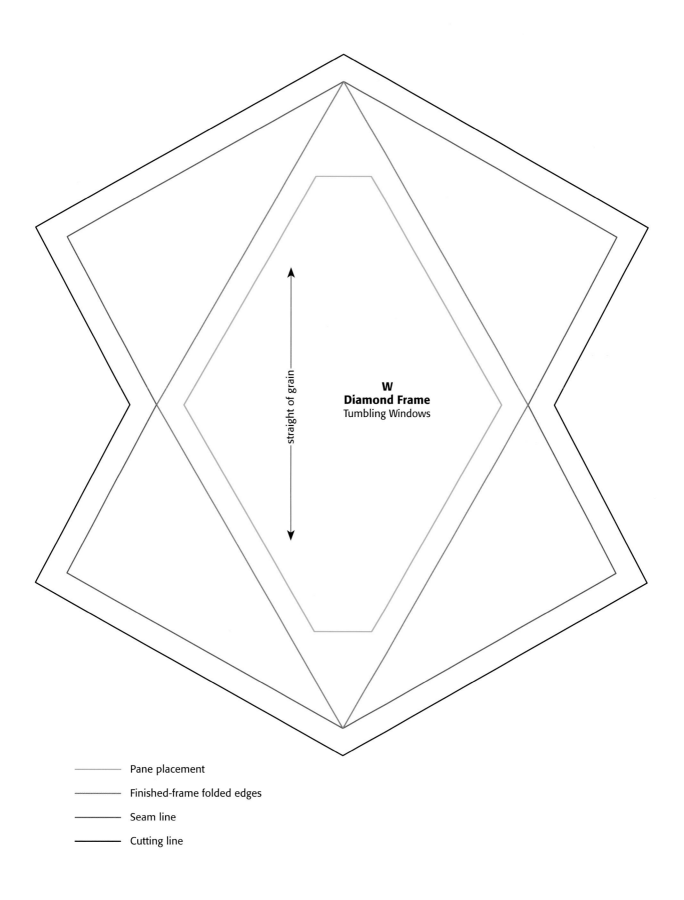

W
Diamond Frame
Tumbling Windows

straight of grain

Pane placement

Finished-frame folded edges

Seam line

Cutting line

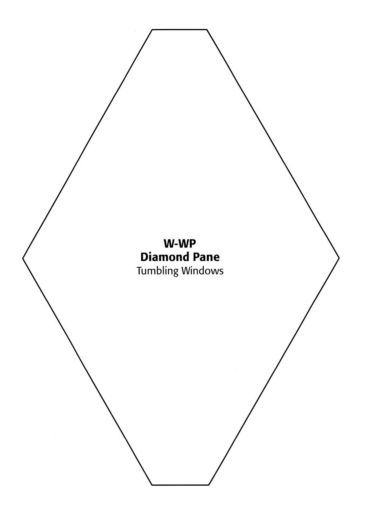

W-WP
Diamond Pane
Tumbling Windows

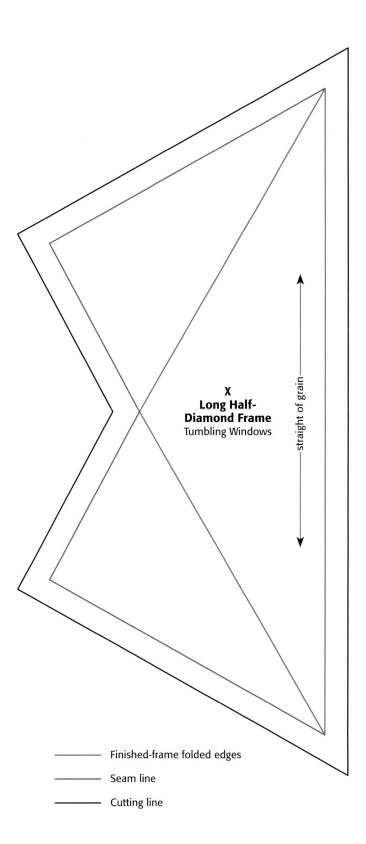

X
Long Half-
Diamond Frame
Tumbling Windows

straight of grain

Finished-frame folded edges

Seam line

Cutting line

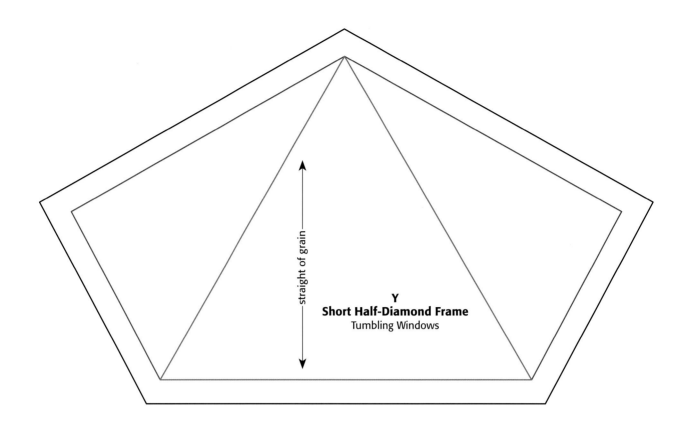

straight of grain

Y
Short Half-Diamond Frame
Tumbling Windows

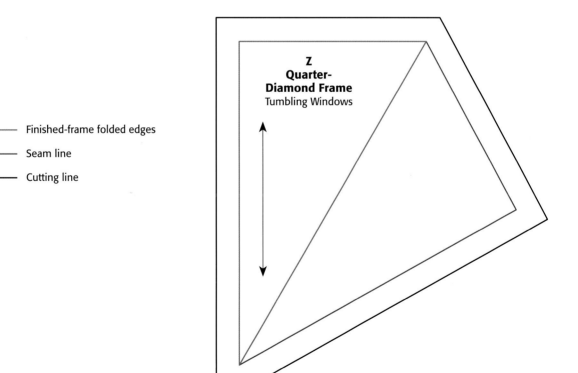

Z
Quarter-
Diamond Frame
Tumbling Windows

Finished-frame folded edges

Seam line

Cutting line

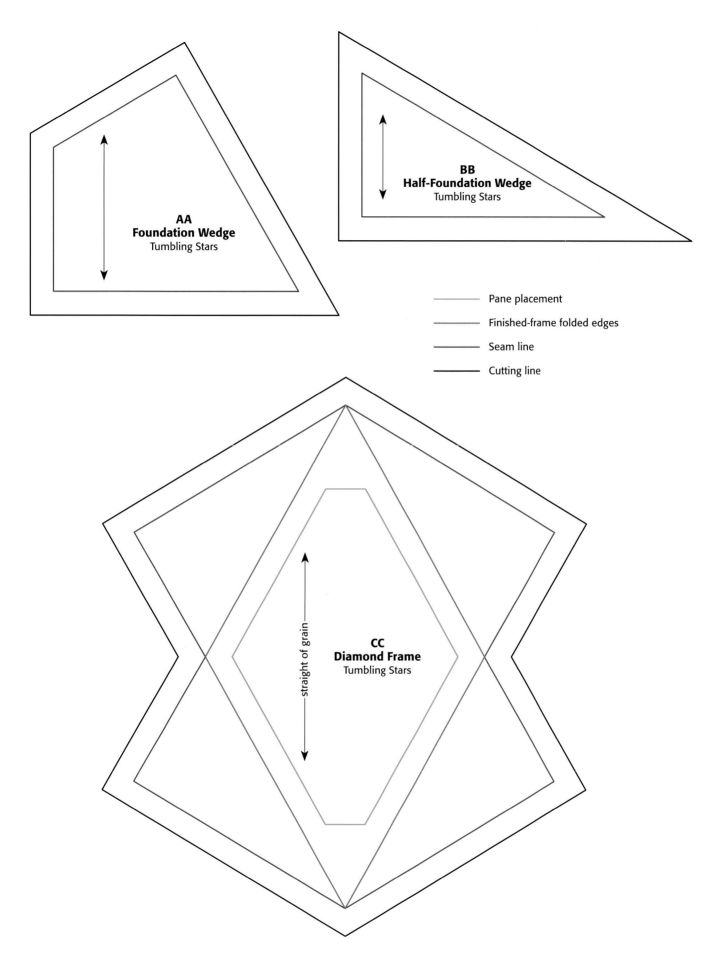

**AA
Foundation Wedge**
Tumbling Stars

**BB
Half-Foundation Wedge**
Tumbling Stars

Pane placement

Finished-frame folded edges

Seam line

Cutting line

straight of grain

**CC
Diamond Frame**
Tumbling Stars

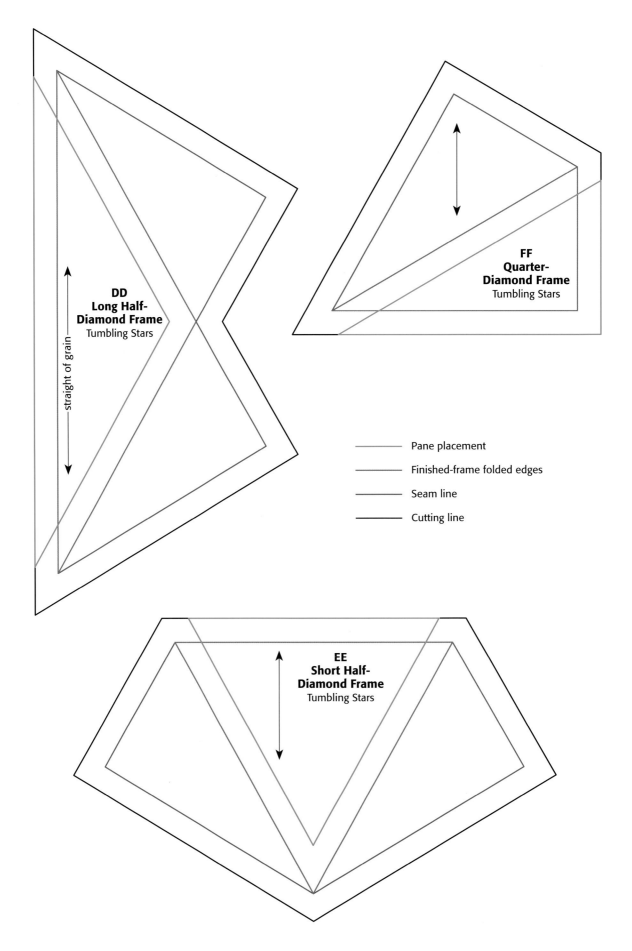

**DD
Long Half-
Diamond Frame**
Tumbling Stars

straight of grain

**FF
Quarter-
Diamond Frame**
Tumbling Stars

Pane placement

Finished-frame folded edges

Seam line

Cutting line

**EE
Short Half-
Diamond Frame**
Tumbling Stars

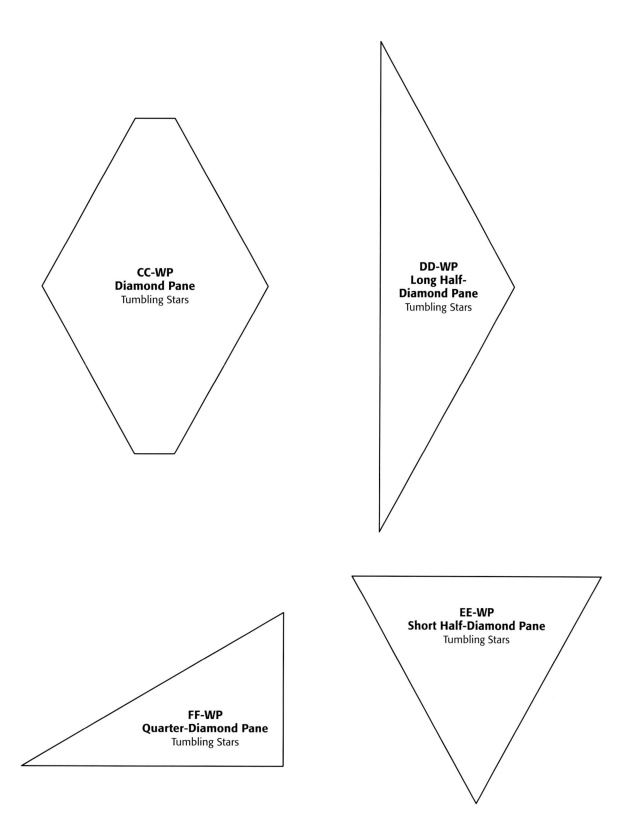

CC-WP
Diamond Pane
Tumbling Stars

DD-WP
Long Half-
Diamond Pane
Tumbling Stars

EE-WP
Short Half-Diamond Pane
Tumbling Stars

FF-WP
Quarter-Diamond Pane
Tumbling Stars

ABOUT THE AUTHOR

SEWING HAS BEEN a passion of Shelley Swanland since she was a child. She would fashion doll clothes by hand from scraps and later sewed her own clothes. Quilting was a natural transition. She has been a member of SLO Quilters, Inc., since 1989. The twin passions of quilting and wearable art keep her busy creating, competing, and teaching. She makes her home on the central coast of California.